The Lotus and the Artichoke

MALAYSIA

A culinary adventure with over 70 vegan recipes

Justin P. Moore

ventil

The Lotus and the Artichoke
MALAYSIA – A culinary adventure with over 70 vegan recipes

The information in this book is true and complete to the best of my knowledge. This book is intended only as an informal guide for those wishing to know more about cooking, food, and travel. In no way is this book intended to replace, countermand, or conflict with advice given to you by a physician. Likewise, caution and common sense should be used in selecting travel destinations and activities. The information in this book is general and offered without any guarantee on the part of the author and publisher. The author and publisher disclaim all liability in connection with the use of this book.

1st English edition October 2016

Graphic Design, Illustration, Photography © Justin P. Moore
Photographic assistance: Julia Augustin (pgs. 4 & 5)

Edition Kochen ohne Knochen

Printed in Germany

ISBN 978-3-95575-064-0

Ventil Verlag
Boppstr. 25
55118 Mainz
Germany
www.ventil-verlag.de

www.lotusartichoke.com
facebook.com/lotusartichoke
instagram.com/lotusartichoke

THE LOTUS AND THE ARTICHOKE~

MALAYSIA

THAILAND
PENANG
IPOH
MALAYSIA
PULAU
PANGKOR
BATU CAVES
KUALA
LUMPUR
MELAKA
JOHOR
BAHRU
SINGAPORE
INDONESIA

THE LOTUS AND THE ARTICHOKE
BRUNEI
PERMAI
KUCHING
MALAYSIA
BORNEO
INDONESIA

About this Cookbook

In 1999, I was living in an artist studio loft in Philadelphia's Chinatown. I could see Penang, the new restaurant down the street, from my second floor windows. One cool evening, my curiosity steered me through the entrance. The names and descriptions of the dishes intrigued me. The atmosphere and presentation were even more impressive: Waiters dashed from a chaotic kitchen to crowded tables carrying oversized platters with steaming hot, gorgeous food splattered across fresh banana leaves. The colors, smells and sounds were powerful. The place was packed, loud, and electric.

That first Malaysian meal blew me away – Such intensely unique, yet mysteriously familiar flavors! I tasted hints of delightful cuisines I already knew: especially Thai, Vietnamese, Chinese, and Indian. This was just months before my first trip to Asia, but I had fallen in love with Asian cooking long ago.

When I was fifteen, I decided to embrace a vegetarian way of life – for ethical, environmental, and health reasons. Within two years, I transitioned to vegan when the term was mostly unknown. I cooked often for family and friends, and got really into international cuisines, discovering new worlds of flavor, foods, and cooking methods. I dreamed of visiting these places, meeting the people, immersing myself in the cultures, learning new languages, and devouring delicious food together.

I grew up in a family that traveled a lot. My brothers and I spent six years in the Marshall Islands, with many trips to Micronesian and Polynesian islands in the Pacific. World cultures always fascinated me, and I was spellbound by the breathtaking photographs in National Geographic: bustling cities, colorful villages and towns, tribes in traditional dress, luscious rainforests, imposing mountains, and magnificent animals from around our planet.

After high school, I completed a degree in Fine Arts, then worked in Boston and Philadelphia as an artist and designer. My hunger for travel grew. Weekend camping trips or city visits turned to cross-country motorcycle tours. Short travels to Europe became backpacking in Asia for weeks, and then months. I documented my adventures with stories, drawings, and photographs, as I had since I was a kid.

In 2001, full of dreams and ambition, I booked a one-way ticket and intensive German language course and moved to Berlin. I continued cooking, painting, printmaking, designing, photographing, and visiting at least one new country every year.

The Lotus and the Artichoke combines all of these passions. My first cookbook was a collection of vegan recipes, art, photography, and stories inspired by my travels to nearly 40 countries. Following the success of the first book, my partner Julia, our young son Kolja, and I traveled to Mexico, and then Sri Lanka, the subjects of my second and third cookbooks, also published in German and English.

In early 2016, we flew to Kuala Lumpur for a five week journey around Malaysia, Singapore, and Borneo – by bus, train, taxi, boat, and plane. We stayed in city hotels, simple guesthouses, island chalets, and even a jungle treehouse. As always, I found my way into the kitchens of homes and restaurants, cooked with locals, tried so many new dishes and snacks, and filled my journal with notes and pictures. Back in Germany, I spent the next months creating the recipes, artwork, and photography for this book. And here I share with you my inspiration, insights, and memories from the adventures.

Enjoy!

Justin P. Moore
October 2016
Berlin, Germany

Adventures in
MALAYSIA, SINGAPORE & BORNEO

The flight landed in **Kuala Lumpur** and we took a taxi downtown into the city. The driver drove us as far as Chinatown, but couldn't find the address for our place. Confused, he told us to get out. We stumbled around for a few blocks before finding the Winsin hotel. We cleaned up and walked to India town for dinner. When considering destinations for this year's big trip, I was well aware that Malaysia had a significant Indian community and that vegan and vegetarian Indian food would never be far away. The waiter brought our crispy dosas, chutneys, and steaming curries to the table, and we dove in.

That evening we braved the Chinatown market for the first time, packed with fashion, electronics, toys, and bootleg goods from around the world, but mostly factories in neighboring countries. It reminded me of the backpacker ghetto of Khao San Road in Bangkok and crowded markets of Beijing – both charming and disturbing. We explored the city, had fresh juices, walked in the hot sun, and just took in everything. Malaysian food is also renowned for the Chinese influence and likewise large community. There were vegetarian Chinese restaurants and Chinese dishes on menus everywhere. We rode the subway deep beneath the metropolis and emerged at a slick shopping mall with a mind-boggling view of the Petronas Towers, with their trademark connecting bridge, just like on all the postcards.

The impressive Sri Maha Mariamman Hindu temple was near our hotel, so we slipped off our shoes and wandered in to soak in the vibe. It was just like being in South India, but the real taste was yet to come. The next day I took the train by myself out to the Batu Caves to witness the yearly Thaipusam festival. Loud music roared and tens of thousands of pilgrims clambered up the steep steps to the cave temple. Many were in trances and wearing elaborate costumes with ornaments and jewelry that pierced their flesh with hooks and skewers. There were hundreds of vendors offering all kind of snacks for the hungry and spiritual souvenirs for the devout.

Another day, we explored Brickfields, another Indian neighborhood that was every bit as authentic as the one near our hotel. On the map it looked like a 15 minute walk, but it took us almost 2 hours in the heat to get there in the concrete jungle of highways, canals, and bridges – but few pedestrian walkways. After our first mouth-watering Malaysian Banana Leaf meal with my blogger friends Molly and Luane, there was an immense downpour. We took a cab in the rain back to Chinatown.

In the morning, we packed up everything and went to the train station. We wanted to go north, but all the trains were booked out. "What about Singapore?" I asked. Before we knew it we were on a train going seven hours south instead, to the last stop, **Johor Bahru**. It took an hour to cross the border into **Singapore**. We took a bus to Indiatown. It was nearly midnight and the others were in bed, but I was wide awake and hungry. On the streets, I bumped into fellow backpacker Preetam, who'd met on the train. He was also on a late-night dinner mission. We found an all-night Indian restaurant and ordered up two Thali plates of the veg curries and drank chilled coconut water. I walked back to the Madras motel and fell into a deep sleep, despite the thundering Tamil pop tunes from the downstairs disco.

Singapore was a heaven of vegan options. The Indian food was spectacular, the Chinese food was some of the best I'd had since Shanghai, and the culinary fusion of international styles was phenomenal. During the day we explored the city and visited landmarks, weaving through crowds of schoolchildren and armies of holiday makers with selfie sticks. I shared lunch with a local pen pal, and then went for dinner with an old friend and former roomate from my Boston days. After hours of catching-up, nostalgic stories, and lots of laughter, I practically forgot the decade and country of the present.

We flew to **Penang**, to avoid the immigration circus going overland via Kuala Lumpur. Our cab drove us to **Georgetown**, but the evening traffic was at a standstill. Sixty minutes later, we made the last two blocks to the Cintra Heritage Home, straight out of the 19th century, but only a steps away from the action. The food in Penang was out of this world and the atmosphere charged with life and emotion. The Chinese restaurants were exceptional, the Indian places were also insanely great. The local street food and snacks were fun, too. Day after day, night after night, we ate our way through every plant-focused restaurant we could find. And there was always another one. We checked out Chinese palaces, and rode in a decked-out cycle rickshaw. We drank cold coconut juice, tried Malaysian iced drinks and desserts, and even had fantastic Japanese food. I met the owner of Sushi Kitchen, and she drove me to her friend's restaurant to meet the crew. They made a big meal just for me and we talked for hours.

In Penang I discovered steamed Otak-Otak, Popiah rolls, sensational Laksa noodle soup, and really began to explore Malaysian culinary fusion. The flavors were intense and complex: sweet and tangy, but also spicy and powerful. I took notes of all the new delights. We rode up Penang Hill in a funicular and enjoyed the view. After another day of fantastic Indian food, including the steaming Punjabi Sizzler platter and Indochinese Gobi 65, it was time to pack up. We had spent a week in Penang, but I could've stayed another two, just for the food.

The morning ferry took us close to the bus station. We got fresh fruit and snacks for the ride to Lamut, and then another small boat to the island of **Pulau Pangkor**. We arrived in the village of **Teluk Nipah**, which had a few places to stay near the beach. We checked into a cute wooden chalet from the family-run Ombak Inn and ventured out to the main street with a view of the coast and a string of sit-down cheap eateries and street food stalls. Over the next few days we returned over and over again to Restaurant No. 7, where I got to know the chef and owner, and got to go in the kitchen with him. He showed me how to make Sayur Campur, Kangkung Goreng, and other classics. We swam in the sea and played at a modest beach a short walk uphill toward the jungle and Buddhist rock temple, with an odd campground at the base, with tents and cabins of students on island adventure get-away trips.

It was the Chinese New Year holiday week. every evening the island became a carnival of Malaysian locals and primarily Asian tourists. We met a Dutch family and twice snuck our way into the pool of their fancier resort down the street from where we were staying. After swimming, we brought the kids to eat delicious rotis, grilled vegetable-stuffed flatbreads, and vegetable fried noodles and rice from our favorite beach restaurant. I swam from the beach to the tiny, uninhabited neighboring island. I rested in the shade, and then paddled back to the main island. I hadn't swam so much in the sea since Mexico, two years before, where surfing in strong currents got me in great shape. Living in the Marshall Islands as a kid taught me to appreciate and respect deep water and waves. It thrills me, yet sometimes scares me a little, to be so far out from shore.

After several days we were ready to move on. We took the ferry back to the mainland and then a local bus to **Ipoh**, a city with its own emerging cultural and culinary scenes. As in Penang, street art, street food, fine dining, night life and good times are on the rise. The city felt sleepy to me; perhaps everyone really was still just waking up from a week of Chinese New Year celebrations, but there was just an energy or inspiration that was absent.

We took an excursion to the Ling Sen Tong cave temple, which ended up being much more amusement park-like than spiritual. As lunch time grew near, and my stomach started rumbling, I found a sign outside of the old temple complex which promised "Vegetarian Restaurant!" I walked down the long, dusty corridor and came into a surreal dining room with low ceilings, small windows, and empty tables. Was it closed? Was it still a restaurant? A face emerged from the shadows, from what might have been a kitchen. A waiter? A cook? I greeted him and made the universal gestures for I'm Hungry and

Do You Have Food, first patting my belly, and then shoveling invisible bites into my mouth. He looked confused, but then his face lit up, and the fetched a wrinkled sheet of paper that must've been a menu. Except for the numbers, I couldn't make sense of it. And if the numbers were prices, they must've been for elaborate meals for entire tour groups or giant families. The charades were going nowhere fast, and I didn't want to risk ordering a five course meal for ten people, so we politely excused ourselves and found a ride back to town.

By contrast, the Chinese vegetarian restaurants downtown were more accessible and had decent food. The Indian restaurants were quite good. We enjoyed excellent Roti Canai breakfasts at the old school diner on the corner. Still, nothing I tried in Ipoh really blew me away as had happened almost every day in KL, Singapore, and Penang. When I feel these heavy comparisons and judgements setting in, and a place feels off, there are two things to do: Dedicate more time and focus there, or just move on, and appreciate the ride to something else.

I went to the train station to book the two hour journey for the following day. It was a circus inside! We'd made the same mistake again. Even for such a short trip, everything was booked out for days. I was baffled by how different the trains in Malaysia are from other parts of Asia – and from train travel in past decades. I'm used to last minute bookings and abundant tickets, and the possiblity to just ride without a seat for an hour or two. The trains here were ultra-modern and the tickets very affordable, and understandably desirable. Combined with the holiday traffic of everyone going home, this led to chaos and confusion. In Sri Lanka and India I experienced that a lot of taxi drivers are willing to take you a few hours' drive for totally reasonable prices if they're charmed, curious, or just bored. But that just wasn't happening here this time. I had to find another solution: an early morning bus from the massive suburban bus terminal, which meant waking at the crack of dawn and a mini taxi journey.

The return to the cosmopolitan flash, fun, and hustle of KL was refreshing. We stayed in a small room at the Hotel 1915 on the same noisy side street of our beloved South Indian eatery, Sangeetha Veg Restaurant. This meant dosas and idlys for breakfast, an afternoon out and about, and Indian and Indochinese dishes for dinner, followed by fresh sweets. But we were just passing through this time. The following day we flew to **Borneo**, fulfilling another of my childhood travel dreams.

Like most people, I always imagine what places will be like before I arrive. With **Kuching**, things were so different than the picture in my head. In the age of the internet, it's simple and tempting to preview far-away places. This time, I'd intentionally only read about the place, and didn't look online to prepare myself. Kuching was an odd mix of Borneo tourism, old historic town feel, billowing incense temples, new shopping malls, and quaint folk museums with cosy parks and trails. I met Boy Skrang and Baxx Jordan, world-famous tattoo artists. I got a traditional Borneo hand-tapped tattoo on my leg, the design a mix of Iban and Polynesian elements, a tribute to my younger years. The Chinese vegetarian buffet lunches at Zhun San Yen were incredible, and many dishes there inspired recipes for this book. I also had some terrific noodle soups at Life Cafe just around the corner from the guesthouse.

I had hoped to travel to Miri, and from there to the famous, magnificent caves at Mulu National Park, or which I had seen in film documentaries and photos. But visiting the slightly-less famous Fairy Cave close to Kuching didn't require any 20 hour bus rides, jungle river boat rides, or multiple flights. It was a small compromise: The tunnels and hollows in the earth were indeed impressive, and a highlight of the whole trip to Malaysia. It was an adventure to climb and wind the subterranean paths with a headlamp. For most of the day we had the whole cave to ourselves. Water trickled down melodically from the ceiling and light from the heavens beamed in from the mouth of the cavern. One day I hope to return and explore Mulu and more famous caves of Borneo.

MELAKA

We rode a few hours north to the rainforest of **Permai**, and checked into a jungle treehouse high above the earth on wooden stilts. It was unquestionably one of the coolest places I've ever stayed. Down the trail was a dining pavilion where we ate made to order rice and noodle dishes under a thatched roof. The most memorable food was at the Sarawak cultural village. I met the chefs and they taught me how to make Kelabit Mango Salad and shared with me a cookbook of tribal cuisine. We explored the traditional villages, watched a concert, took lots of photos, and snacked on little fried cakes. Later, we hiked to the natural swimming pool and further up the trail to a private beach. There was a small cluster of eateries just outside the village. We drank fresh juices and ate more fried rice and noodles, the classic standby served street food style: spicy with lots of sauces to add as you like. After a few nights we got a ride back to the guesthouse in Kuching. I collected woven and wooden kitchen and dining items and some tribal art from the markets, and we had a comically unauthentic Middle Eastern meal at a Lebanese restaurant we tried out of curiosity. We recovered with more noodle soups and Chinese buffets in the neighborhood, and I hung out with Baxx and Boy Skrang some more.

We flew back to Kuala Lumpur, and took the bus from the airport south several hours to **Malacca**, to indulge in great food, fun conversation, and a week of hanging out with my travel pal Bram from NYC, whom I try to meet every year in a new place – preferably one with Indian food. He had suggested Malacca, having been there over a decade ago, anxious to see how it had developed. Our first dinner destination was, of course, the local Selvam restaurant, where Indian-Malaysian curries, rice, and chutneys were shoveled out of buckets on to fresh banana leaves right in front of our faces. We went for dinner almost every night, and each time they had new curries featuring all kinds of local vegetables, and dozens of dosas and other unforgetable South Indian eats to choose from.

Malacca had a decent selection of vegetarian restaurants, so we went to all of them, and then back to most again, too. We rode the corny, garishly decorated cycle rickshaws, which Kolja loved. We explored the waterfront, and hiked around hillside colonial Portuguese ruins. We ventured across and beyond the old town many times, to stroll aside the waterways, through the winding alleys, down dry, dusty lanes, and found world-class Malaysian and Chinese vegan restaurants. I met the cooks and their dishes: Spicy Tempeh Cubes, rich soups, as well as fresh and tangy Rojak fruit salad. At the crowded Man Yuan Fang family restaurant, I ate the best Chinese food since Singapore. Their Veg KFC, fried faux-chicken, was so good I ordered seconds, and took notes to recreate the recipe back home .

At the night market we ate snacks like fried bananas from the street vendors and watched the crowds. On the weekend, the old town was flooded with cars and motorcycles cruising the small streets and drag racing down the long, straightaways into the early hours. I cooked simple breakfasts and lunches in the shared kitchen of the inn, and we ate at the family table with other guests, or in the garden watching colorful birds in the mango trees overhead.

The final two days of the Malaysia journey we spent back in Kuala Lumpur. We got returned to Hotel 1915, and began the Indian food ritual again, getting smiles and handshakes every time we entered the restaurants. Bram flew back to India, where he planned to spend a few months. We ate more dosas in his honor. After some gift shopping, more market strolls, and a haircut at a cute barber shop in Chinatown, it was time to pack up. The five weeks had flown by, and I wished we had a few more.

In the Kitchen

Malaysian cooking is a terrific fusion of cultures, flavors, and techniques. The region is famous for its own unique, varied flavors, traditions and dishes shared with neighboring Indonesia and Thailand, and the culinary gifts of generations of Chinese and South Indian communities. The colonial history and extensive trade routes through the region have also massively influenced the food and flavors.

The recipes in this book are a collection of vegan delights inspired by my travels in over 50 countries, focusing on the time I spent recently in Malaysia, Singapore, and Borneo. I have created recipes which use ingredients, spices, and cooking methods which are practical and available beyond Asia. Most Asian grocers and the international section of larger supermarkets, both organic and conventional, will have everything you need. The recipes frequently mention substitutions for less common ingredients as well as ways to simplify preparation and cooking. If you're new to the kitchen, or unfamiliar with Asian cooking, follow recipes closely. After some practice, feel free to experiment and be creative. Cook with passion, feel inspired, explore new tastes, ingredients, and methods. Above all, enjoy!

Fruit & Vegetables

I recommend fresh and organic ingredients. In most cases, frozen berries, fruit, and greens (spinach, beans, etc.) provide great results, too. Jackfruit is great if you can get it fresh, but canned jackfruit from the Asian shop is fine. Use green, young (unsweetened) jackfruit for savory dishes. More commonly found yellow, ripe (sweetened) jackfruit works for savory recipes, but is softer and fruitier. If using canned ingredients, use organic, unsweetened, unsalted, and without additives, whenever possible. Fresh coconut is unbeatable for grated coconut. Shake coconuts before buying: If you don't hear water sloshing around, it's probably rotten. Quality, dried (desiccated) grated coconut works well, too. Soak in hot water prior to use. If using store-bought coconut milk, buy without additives and preservatives. Banana leaves are often available fresh or frozen at Asian markets.

Spices, Herbs, Chilies

Freshly ground spices always taste better. This is especially true for grinding your own whole black pepper, Szechuan pepper, coriander, and cumin. Less common spices, like fresh (or dried) curry leaves, fresh turmeric, black mustard seeds, and asafoetida (hing) – all usually easy to find at most Asian markets – upgrade the authentic flavor of your dishes, especially with Indian dishes. For Chinese dishes, homemade 5 Spice Powder (page 27) is amazing and tastes much better than store-bought. Purchased spice mixes save time, but taste less intense and usually steer flavors to the west. Store spices in airtight containers in a cool, dry place. Replace opened and home-ground spices within a few months. Old spices taste drab and ruin dishes.

I prefer fresh herbs over dried. Curry leaves, dried or fresh, are a must for authentic Indian flavor. Pandan (also known as pandanus) leaves are not absolutely necessary, but add a nice touch. Blend fresh pandan leaves with water, then strain and discard the solids to make a colorful, fragrant green juice with a light, sweet vanilla flavor. If you can't get pandan leaves for savory recipes, omit them, or substitute bay leaves. Fresh lemongrass is best, but ground, dried lemongrass works. Lime or lemon zest is a fair substitute. Galangal brings unique, woody flavor to dishes. Ginger is similar, but not the same. If unavailable fresh, use 1 tsp minced galangal or ginger from a jar for every 1/2 in (1 cm) fresh.

Many recipes call for fresh, large, red chilies (e.g. cayenne), which are less hot than small chilies (e.g. bird's eye), dried or fresh. Like things hot? Add 1 or 2 chopped red or green chilies to your dishes. Less heat: Use ground (sweet) paprika in place of chili powder and remove seeds from fresh chilies. Paprika is also great for adding a deep red hue to dishes, such as roasted jackfruit and coconut sambal.

Sauces & Soup Stock

As with dry spice mixes, store-bought chutneys, sauces, and spice pastes are quick and easy, but I encourage experimenting with making your own. Hoisin sauce, Sambal Oelek, Sriracha, and Kecap Manis (sweet dark soy sauce) are exceptions I might grab at the store. It's also possible to use store-bought curry paste (check ingredients carefully), if you don't want to make your own.

I recommend quality Japanese soy sauce, such as Shoyu or Tamari. Avoid cheap soy sauce (especially with flavor enhancers, artificial colors, preservatives, etc.) and you'll get better results with your cooking. Many traditional recipes use fish sauce, but good soy sauce is always a reasonable substitute. I created a mildly pungent Vegan Fish Sauce (page 29) for obtaining authentic flavors.

Soups are improved by making your own fresh soup stock. I have provided many recipes for delicious soup stocks and vegetable broths. Make just what you need, or make extra and freeze the rest.

Tofu, Soymeats & Seitan

If you want to replace seitan or soymeat (TVP) with tofu, use extra firm, organic tofu. Press out extra moisture by wrapping the block in a kitchen towel and putting cutting boards on top for 20–30 min. Smoked tofu is also fun for curries, stir-fry recipes, and savory fillings, including for Bao and Wontons. Tofu, soymeat, and seitan can be replaced in most recipes with vegetables such as mushrooms, cauliflower, and root vegetables.

Nuts & Oils

Candlenuts (Kemiri) are used often in Malaysian and Indonesia spice pastes to intensify and compliment flavors. They are available at Asian shops, and should first be soaked, then blended with other spices and cooked. Substitute cashews or brazil nuts for similar results. For Asian cooking, I prefer neutral tasting vegetable oil, such as canola oil, especially for wok cooking and deep frying. Sunflower oil also works well, as does peanut oil, with a slightly nuttier flavor. Experiment with coconut oil, especially for sweet recipes. Refined coconut oil has a subtler taste, but unrefined (virgin) coconut oil is wonderful, too. Sesame oil adds additional flavor, but should be used sparingly.

Flour & Grains

For most recipes, I use all-purpose (type 550), unbleached wheat flour. I sometimes blend in some whole wheat flour to increase nutritional value. Most recipes will work (with minor adjustments) with spelt flour. Especially with rice flour and chickpea flour, be aware that imported Asian varieties are usually more finely ground and work better than organic and conventional flours. Grinding your own flour with the dry container of a high-powered blender is possible. Be ready to adjust amounts in recipes depending on the texture and grind. I use quality (not cheap) basmati rice, Thai jasmine rice, and brown rice. Rinse and drain rice well before cooking.

Sweeteners & Salt

Palm syrup is used often in Malaysian cooking, as is palm (coconut) sugar. When practical and affordable, I use both, preferring organic and fair-trade. Agave syrup, brown rice syrup, and unrefined (raw) sugar work fine, too. I avoid refined sweeteners, but occasionally use brown sugar. In recipes with lemon or lime juice, vinegar, or other sour ingredients, such as tamarind paste, I often add some sweetness to balance flavors. I use sea salt or pink (Himalayan) salt. The most satisfying dishes typically work with an intricate balance of sweet, sour, savory (umami), bitter, and salty tastes. When adjusting recipes to taste, consider which flavors to intensify or compliment.

Weights & Measurements

For my cookbooks, I use a combination of American and metric measurements. Measurements have been tested and determined for both. When creating and refining recipes, I measure both volume and weight. I do not sift flour; Flour measurements are based on scoop & level and weight approximation.

These recipes are not exact formulas for perfection. They are meant as guidelines, instructions, and inspiration. Stray from the recipe if you want to use more or less of ingredients if you feel confident. Enjoy yourself and figure out what works best for you.

Kitchen Appliances, Tools, Cookware

I recommend investing in a good blender. I use my Vitamix high-powered blender every day, for smoothies, sauces, and desserts. However, these recipes have been tested with and are possible with a simple, inexpensive blender, too. A small food processor is very helpful for blending sauces, spice pastes, chutneys, chopping tomatoes, and puréeing small batches of ingredients.

I use a small coffee grinder for spices, nuts, and seeds, but also go old school sometimes with a heavy duty mortar and pestle. I do have a few expensive knives, but have learned over the years to survive with whatever is available in the kitchen.

A set of quality nonstick pots and pans with lids is excellent. A well-seasoned cast iron wok or quality nonstick wok is essential for Asian cooking. For crêpes, pancakes, and roti a large nonstick crêpe or chapatti pan (tawa) or seasoned, heavy, cast iron frying pan is highly recommended. For roasting small batches of seeds and nuts I use a mini nonstick frying pan.

Following Recipes

The recipe descriptions and instructions are written as simple and clear as possible. My photographs give an idea of how your creation may turn out, and how to present it. Don't be concerned if your dish looks different! I encourage experimentation, improvement, and variation with these recipes.

Estimated cooking times do not include long periods of soaking, extended cooling or refrigeration, letting batter sit or dough raise, etc. Recipes that involve idle time are marked with +.

Portions and serving estimates will give you an idea of the recipe's yield. Double or halve recipes as needed. Most recipes are intended for 2 to 3 servings, others make enough for 4 or more. My portions run a bit small: particularly for dishes served along with others. If you're only cooking one dish for more than two people, keep this in mind.

Vegan Malaysian Kitchen Inventory:

Fruits & Vegetables
apples
bananas
bean sprouts
beets
bok choy (pak choi)
cabbage
carrots
coconut
cucumber
eggplant (aubergine)
green beans
kohlrabi
lemons
limes
mango
pineapple
potatoes
shallots
spinach
spring onions
sweet potatoes
tomatoes
zucchini (courgette)

tempeh
tofu (firm & smoked)
seitan

Fresh Herbs & Spices
chilies (cayenne & bird's eye)
coriander
curry leaves
galangal
garlic
ginger
lemongrass
mint leaves
pandan leaves
parsley
Thai basil
turmeric root

Frozen
banana leaves
kefir lime leaves
wonton wrappers

Spices & Seasonings (dried)
asafoetida (hing) powder
bay leaves
black pepper (whole & ground)
cardamom
cinnamon (whole & ground)
cloves
coriander seeds (whole & ground)
cumin (whole & ground)
curry leaves
fenugreek seeds
fennel seeds
kala namak (black salt)
mustard seeds (black/brown)
paprika (ground)
red chilies
sea salt
star anise (whole)
szechuan peppercorns
turmeric (ground)

Nuts & Seeds
candlenuts (kemari)
cashews
flax seeds (ground)
peanuts
sesame seeds
walnuts

Rice & Noodles
basmati rice
brown rice
jasmine rice
flat rice noodles
udon noodles
mee (wheat) noodles
vermicelli (rice) noodles

Flours
all-purpose (unbleached) flour
chickpea flour (besan)
glutinous rice flour (Asian)
rice flour (Asian)

Sauces & Pastes
soy sauce (Shoyu/Tamari)
chili sauce (Srirachi)
curry paste
Hoisin sauce
Kecap Manis (sweet soy sauce)
peanut butter
tamarind paste (seedless)
Sambal Oelek
tomato paste (concentrate)

Sweetners
agave syrup (dark)
brown rice syrup
brown sugar
palm (coconut) sugar
palm (coconut) syrup
unrefined raw sugar

Oils
coconut oil (unrefined)
margarine (Alsan/Earth Balance)
peanut oil
sesame oil
vegetable oil (canola, sunflower)

Vinegar
apple vinegar
rice vinegar

Other
baking powder
coconut cream
coconut milk (min. 60%)
corn starch
lentils (red, yellow)
seaweed (Nori & Kombu)
shiitake mushrooms (dried)
soy chunks (TVP)
soy milk
soy flour
tofu beancurd skins (sheets)
fried onions (dried)
jackfruit (green & yellow, canned)
lychees (canned)

Hefeflocken
BIOVEGAN
Johannisbrot-kernmehl
Shoyu
KETJAP MANIS

5
FIVE SPICE
·POWDER·

5 Spice Powder
classic Chinese spice mix

makes about 1/4 cup / time 15 min

2 star anise whole
1 tsp cloves whole
1/2 cinnamon stick or **2 large pieces cinnamon bark**
3 tsp Szechuan peppercorns whole
2 tsp fennel seeds

1. Heat a small frying pan on medium heat. Add whole **star anise**, **cloves**, **cinnamon**, and **peppercorns**. Stirring constantly, lightly roast until fragrant, about 3–5 min.
2. Add **fennel** seeds. Continue to roast 2–3 min, stirring constantly. Be careful not to burn spices! Remove from heat immediately if they start to smoke. Remove from heat and allow to cool.
3. Grind to a fine powder with coffee grinder or mortar and pestle. Store in an airtight container in a cool, dark place. Will keep for 3–4 months or longer.

Variations:
6 Spice Powder: Grind with 2–3 tsp coriander seeds. **Peppercorns**: Replace Szechuan peppercorns with whole black pepper, or colored peppercorns.

VEGAN
FISH
SAUCE

Vegan Fish Sauce
for stir-frys & more

makes about 1 2/3 cups / time 50 min

1/2 cup (60 g) fresh pineapple chopped
1 oz (25 g) seaweed (Kombu or Wakame)
1 cup (240 ml) soy sauce (Shoyu)
1 1/2 cup (360 ml) water
1 tsp whole black pepper
2 cloves garlic chopped *optional*
1 in (3 cm) fresh galangal or **ginger** chopped
2 stalks lemongrass chopped
1 tsp coconut sugar *optional*
1/4–1/2 tsp sea salt
2 dried shiitake mushrooms
2 bay leaves

1. Add **all ingredients** to a large pot and bring to boil. Reduce heat to low. Simmer and reduce as desired, stirring occasionally, 30–45 min.
2. Remove from heat. Depending on the saltiness of the seaweed and sweetness of the pineapple, adjust **sugar** and **salt** as needed.
3. Strain liquid into a sealable jar or bottle. Discard solids.
4. Allow to cool. Kept sealed will keep several weeks in fridge.

Rempeh
red curry spice paste

makes about 2/3 cup / time 30 min

5 large (120 g) red chilies chopped
1/3 cup (40 g) candlenuts
2–5 dried small red chilies (e.g. bird's eye chilies)
2 stalks lemongrass finely chopped
3 cloves garlic finely chopped
6 shallots finely chopped
1 in (3 cm) fresh galangal or **ginger** finely chopped
or **1 Tbs minced galangal** or **ginger** (from a jar)
3/4 in (2 cm) fresh turmeric peeled, chopped
or **1 tsp turmeric** ground
2 Tbs coconut sugar or **agave syrup**
2 Tbs lime juice or **lemon juice**
1 tsp fennel seeds
1 Tbs whole coriander seeds or **2 tsp coriander** ground
3–4 Tbs oil as needed

1. Soak **dried chilies** and **candlenuts** in hot water 30 min. Rinse and drain.
2. Lightly roast **coriander** and **fennel seeds** in a small pan on medium heat, until aromatic, 2–3 min. Grind in a coffee grinder or mortar and pestle.
3. Combine **all ingredients** and blend smooth in a small food processor, 30–60 sec, adding **oil** last and gradually as needed to produce smooth paste. Alternately, pound and grind in a mortar and pestle until smooth.
4. Heat small pan on medium heat. Fry blended spice paste, stirring constantly, until it darkens and oil separates, 5–8 min. Remove from heat, allow to cool.
5. Use for making soups, curries, and noodle or rice dishes. Traditionally, many Malaysian noodle soups are served with a spoonful of rempeh paste to stir in yourself. After using, keep remaining spice paste well-sealed in a jar in the fridge.

Variations:
Other nuts: Replace candlenuts with brazil nuts or cashews.

Soup Stock
homemade vegetable broth

makes about 6 cups / time 20 min

2 large carrots
1 small fennel bulb or **1/2 small head cabbage**
2 celery stalks
2 dried shiitake mushrooms
2 bay leaves
1 stalk lemongrass
3/4 in (2 cm) fresh ginger
1/2 tsp whole black pepper
1/2 tsp 5 Spice Powder (page 27)
1/2 tsp sea salt
8 cups (2000 ml) water

1. Add **all ingredients** to a large pot. Bring to boil. Reduce heat to low. Simmer 40–60 min.
2. Strain and discard solids.
3. Use immediately or allow to cool and store well-sealed in the fridge for up to a week. Or pour into a large sealable container, cover, and freeze.

SALADS
& SAUCES

Kelabit Mango Salad
fresh & fruity

serves 2 / time 20 min

1 medium (200 g) mango peeled, chopped
1 shallot finely chopped *optional*
1 small radish finely sliced
1 Tbs lime juice or **lemon juice**
1 Tbs soy sauce (Shoyu) or **Vegan Fish Sauce** (page 29)
1/4 tsp black pepper ground
1/4 tsp sea salt
small bunch celery greens or **fresh parsley leaves** finely chopped, for garnish

1. Toss **all ingredients** except chopped greens in a large bowl.
2. Adjust **salt** and **lime** (or **lemon**) **juice** to taste. Cover and refrigerate until ready to serve.
3. Alternately, arrange in layers in individual bowls.
4. Serve in bowls garnished with chopped **celery greens** or **parsley leaves**.

Variations:
Berry: Add 4–6 thinly sliced strawberries. **Nutty**: Add 1/3 cup (35 g) roasted, crumbled peanuts, cashews, or walnuts.

Shredded Beet Salad
with coconut & tomato

serves 3 to 4 / time 20 min

2 medium (180 g) beets peeled, grated
10–12 (125 g) cherry tomatoes quartered
3/4 cup (75 g) fresh coconut grated
or **1/2 cup (40 g) dried grated coconut + 3 Tbs hot water**
1 Tbs lime juice or **lemon juice**
1/4 tsp black pepper ground
1/4 tsp sea salt
1 tsp agave syrup or **palm syrup**

1. If using dried, grated **coconut**, mix well with hot water and soak 20 min. Drain any excess water.
2. Combine **all ingredients** in a large bowl and mix well.
3. Adjust **lime** (or **lemon**) **juice**, **salt** and **syrup** to taste.

Variations:
Extra Kick: Add grated carrot and radish.

Cucumber Zucchini Noodles
with Orange Chili Dressing

serves 2 to 4 / time 20 min

1 medium (180 g) cucumber spiralized or cut into long, thin strips
1 medium (180 g) zucchino spiralized or cut into long, thin strips
1 small radish finely sliced, for garnish
fresh coriander leaves finely chopped, for garnish

Orange Chili Dressing:

1/2 cup (120 ml) fresh orange juice
1 Tbs lime juice or **lemon juice**
1/2 large red chili chopped
1/2 in (1 cm) fresh ginger chopped
1 Tbs oil
1 tsp sesame oil
1 tsp soy sauce (Shoyu)
1 tsp coconut sugar or **agave syrup** *optional*
1/4 tsp sea salt

1. Blend **all dressing ingredients** in a small food processor or blender until smooth.
2. Spiralize or slice **cucumber** and **zucchini**. Toss strips in a large bowl with dressing.
3. Adjust **salt**, **sugar** (or **syrup**), and **lime** (or **lemon**) **juice** to taste.
4. Garnish with **sliced radish** and fresh chopped **coriander leaves** and serve.

Variations:

Sprouts: Add 1 cup (40 g) bean sprouts or mixed sprouts. **Sliced**: Cut cucumber and zucchini into very thin slices instead of strips or spiralized noodles.

Gado-Gado

tempeh & steamed vegetables with peanut sauce

serves 2 to 4 / time 30 min

7 oz (200 g) tempeh cut in cubes or slices
3 medium (300 g) potatoes
2 cups (200 g) cabbage finely chopped
1 cup (110 g) broccoli chopped
1 large (110 g) carrot sliced thin
3 small (180 g) tomatoes chopped
1 small (80 g) cucumber sliced
2 Tbs coconut oil or **vegetable oil**
1 Tbs lemon juice
1 Tbs soy sauce (Shoyu)
bean sprouts or **mixed sprouts** for garnish

Simple Peanut Sauce:

4 Tbs natural peanut butter
1/2 tsp chili powder or **paprika** ground
2 Tbs sugar or **agave syrup**
2 Tbs soy sauce (Shoyu)
2 Tbs lemon juice
1/4 tsp sea salt as needed
1/4–1/3 cup (60–80 ml) water

1. Cook whole **potatoes** in a pot of boiling water until soft, 15–20 min. Drain and rinse in cold water. Remove and discard peels. Chop in large, bite-size pieces.
2. In a steamer basket or large covered pot with about 1/2 in (1 cm) water, steam chopped **cabbage**, **broccoli**, and **carrot** just until tender, but still crunchy, 5–8 min. Remove from heat.
3. Heat 2 Tbs **oil** in a large frying pan or wok on medium high heat. Add tempeh pieces and fry, stirring frequently, until crispy and scorched on edges, 5–8 min. Add 1 Tbs **lemon juice** and 1 Tbs **soy sauce**. Continue to fry until liquid is absorbed, 2–3 min. Remove from heat.
4. Whisk all **peanut sauce ingredients** in a bowl until smooth, adding **water** last and gradually. Adjust sweetness and saltiness to taste. For a richer, more intense peanut sauce, make and use Saus Kacang (page 51) instead.
5. Arrange steamed **cabbage, broccoli, potatoes**, and **carrots** on plates or in bowls. Top with **tempeh**, **cucumber**, and **tomato**. Drizzle **peanut sauce** over tempeh and vegetables. Garnish with sprouts and serve. Alternately, toss everything including peanut sauce in a large bowl, portion onto plates topped with sprouts and serve.

Variations:

Orange: Add or substitute chopped sweet potatoes. Steam with cabbage, carrots, and broccoli. **Tofu**: Fry 3.5 oz (100 g) tofu cubes along with tempeh. Or replace tempeh with 10.5 oz (300 g) firm tofu. Adjust soy sauce and lemon juice to taste. **Spice Kick**: Fry 1–2 chopped shallots and garlic cloves, with 1/2 tsp each: ground coriander, pepper, chili powder in oil 2–3 min before adding tempeh pieces.

Rojak
fruity salad with sweet & tangy dressing

serves 3 to 4 / time 30 min

2 medium (300 g) apples (e.g. Granny Smith, Fiji) chopped or sliced
2 cups (300 g) pineapple chopped
1 medium large (250 g) kohlrabi, jicama or **turnip** chopped
1 medium (250 g) cucumber chopped or sliced
2–3 Tbs sesame seeds lightly roasted

rojak dressing:

2 shallots chopped
2 cloves garlic chopped
1 stalk lemongrass chopped
3/4 in (2 cm) fresh galangal or **ginger** chopped
1 large red chili chopped
2 Tbs soy sauce (Shoyu)
1 tsp tamarind paste (seedless)
3 Tbs coconut sugar or **agave syrup**
1 Tbs rice vinegar
1 Tbs lime juice or **lemon juice**
1/2 tsp sea salt
1/2 cup (120 ml) water

1. Arrange chopped **apples**, **pineapple**, **kohlrabi** (or other root vegetable), and **cucumber** on a large plate or combine in a large bowl.
2. Combine and blend all **dressing ingredients** in a small food processor or blender until smooth, adding **water** last and gradually.
3. Heat a small pot on medium heat. Bring blended dressing ingredients to a low boil, stirring constantly. Reduce heat to medium low. Simmer, stirring constantly, gradually reducing, until sauce darkens and thickens, 6–10 min. Remove from heat and allow to cool.
4. Serve salad with dressing in a separate bowl, poured over chopped fruit and vegetables, or mix and combine dressing and chopped ingredients in a large bowl before serving.
5. Top with **sesame seeds**. Serve.

Variation:

Less Heat: Replace large red chili with 1 small plum tomato.

Acar
traditional pickled vegetables

serves 3 to 4 / time 20 min +

1 cup (125 g) cabbage chopped
1 medium (80 g) carrot cut in thin strips
1 cup (100 g) green beans chopped
1/2 medium (90 g) cucumber cut in thin strips
1 Tbs oil
1 clove garlic finely chopped
1 in (3 cm) fresh ginger finely chopped
3 Tbs rice vinegar
1/2 cup (120 ml) water
2 tsp sugar
1/2 tsp sea salt

1. Heat **oil** in a large pot or wok on medium heat. Add chopped **garlic** and **ginger**. Fry, stirring constantly until aromatic, 2–3 min.
2. Mix in **vinegar**, **water**, **sugar**, and **salt**. Stir well. Bring to low boil.
3. Add chopped **cabbage**, **beans**, and **carrot**. Simmer on low, stirring regularly, 2–3 min.
4. Add **cucumber strips**. Stir well. Remove from heat. Cover. Allow to cool.
5. Serve at room temperature or moderately chilled.

Variations:
No Garlic: Substitute 1 tsp mustard seeds (yellow or brown) for chopped garlic. Fry with ginger.

Urap
traditional warm salad with coconut & spices

serves 3 to 4 / time 25 min

2 cups (220 g) cabbage finely chopped
1 medium (100 g) carrot chopped
1 cup (110 g) green beans chopped
1 cup (50 g) bean sprouts
2–3 Tbs water
3/4 cup (75 g) fresh coconut grated
or **1/2 cup (40 g) dried grated coconut + 3 Tbs hot water**
2 Tbs vegetable oil
1 small or **large red chili** finely chopped
1 shallot finely chopped
1 clove garlic finely chopped
2 Tbs lemon juice or **lime juice**
1 tsp tamarind paste (seedless)
1 Tbs coconut sugar or **agave syrup**
1 tsp chili powder or **paprika** ground
3/4 tsp sea salt

1. If using dried, grated **coconut**, combine well with hot **water** and soak 15 min.
2. Heat **oil** in a medium frying pan on medium heat. Add chopped **red chili**, **shallot**, and **garlic**. Fry 2–3 min, stirring constantly.
3. Add **coconut**, **lemon** (or **lime**) **juice**, **tamarind paste**, **coconut sugar** (or **syrup**), **chili powder** (or **paprika**), and **salt**. Mix well. Fry 3 min, stirring regularly. Remove from heat.
4. Heat 2 Tbs **water** in a large pot on medium heat. Add chopped **cabbage** and **carrots**. Cover and steam 5 min.
5. Add **green beans**, **bean sprouts**, and another 1 Tbs **water**, if needed. Stir. Cover and continue to steam just until vegetables soften but still have some crunch, about 3–4 min. Remove from heat.
6. Add **coconut** and **spices** to large pot with vegetables. Combine well. Cover until ready to serve.

Variation:
Nuts: Add 1/3 cup (45 g) roasted, crumbled peanuts or cashews. **Spice Kick**: Add 1/2 tsp each ground black pepper, coriander, and more paprika and/or chili powder.

Serunding Kelapa
roasted, grated coconut, peanuts & spices

makes about 3/4 cup / time 20 min

1/2 cup (45 g) fresh coconut grated
or **1/3 cup (25 g) dried grated coconut + 2 Tbs hot water**
1/4 cup (35 g) peanuts coarsely crumbled
1 shallot finely chopped
1/2 in (1 cm) fresh ginger
1/4 tsp cumin ground
1/4 tsp coriander ground
1/4 tsp black pepper ground
1/2 tsp paprika ground
1 tsp coconut sugar
1 tsp tamarind paste (seedless)
1 tsp lime juice or **lemon juice**

1. If using **dried coconut**, first mix well with 2 Tbs **hot water** in a bowl. Cover and soak 10 min.
2. Heat a medium frying pan on medium heat. Add crumbled **peanuts**. Dry roast, stirring frequently, until golden brown and spots start to form, 3–5 min. Do not burn.
3. Add ground **cumin**, **coriander**, **black pepper**, and **paprika**. Combine well. Continue to dry roast until fragrant, turning and mixing constantly, 1–2 min.
4. Add grated **coconut**, chopped **shallots**, **ginger**, **sugar**, **tamarind**, and **lime** (or **lemon**) **juice**. Mix well. Continue to cook, stirring frequently, until richly aromatic and coconut begins to brown, 3–5 min. Remove from heat. Cover until ready to serve.
5. Serve as garnish or side dish with vegetables, curries, rice, etc.

Variations:
Hotter: Add 1 large red chili, finely chopped and 1/2 tsp chili powder along with coconut and shallots.

Sambal Belacan
tangy & sweet chili sauce

makes 2/3 cup / time 20 min

2–3 Tbs vegetable oil
5 large (90 g) red chilies chopped
2 cloves garlic chopped
1 Tbs soy sauce (Shoyu)
1 Tbs rice vinegar
1 Tbs lime juice or **lemon juice**
1 Tbs coconut sugar
1/4 tsp sea salt

1. Blend **all ingredients** in a small food processor or blender until smooth, adding more **oil** (or some water) as needed.
2. Heat a small frying pan on medium heat. Add blended spice paste to pan and fry, stirring regularly, until sauce darkens, thickens, and oil separates, 8–12 min.
3. Serve as a condiment or dipping sauce with snacks, rice dishes, etc.

Variations:
Mild: Substitute 3 or 4 chopped cherry tomatoes for 3 or 4 large red chilies. Adjust cooking time as needed, possibly adding 3–5 min. **Crazy Heat**: Soak 2 or 3 small dried, red chilies 10 min in hot water. Discard water. Blend soaked chilies with other ingredients.

Saus Kacang
epic peanut sauce

makes about 1 1/2 cups / time 20 min

1/3 cup (45 g) peanuts
2 tsp vegetable oil
1 shallot chopped
2 cloves garlic chopped
1 stalk lemongrass chopped
1/2 in (1 cm) fresh ginger chopped
1 large red chili chopped
1 small red or **green chili** chopped *optional*
2 Tbs soy sauce (Shoyu)
2 Tbs lemon juice
2–3 Tbs coconut sugar or **brown sugar**
1 tsp tamarind paste (seedless)
3/4 tsp sea salt
1/2 cup (120 ml) coconut milk
1/4–1/2 cup (60–120 ml) water as needed

1. Heat **oil** in a small frying pan on medium high heat. Add **peanuts**, chopped **shallots**, **garlic**, **lemongrass**, **ginger**, and **chilies**. Fry, stirring constantly, until peanuts are deep golden brown and shallots are soft, 4–7 min. Remove from heat. Let cool 5 min.
2. Transfer peanuts and spices to a small food processor or blender and add **soy sauce**, **lemon juice**, **sugar**, **tamarind paste**, **salt**, and **coconut milk**. Pulse several times, then blend until mostly smooth. Gradually add **water** as needed and blend to desired consistency and thickness.
3. Sauce thickens as it cools, especially in the fridge. Stir in more water to thin, if desired.
4. Serve with Gado-Gado (page 41) or Satay Skewers (page 73).

Pineapple Pepper Chutney
spicy, sweet & sour sauce

makes about 1 1/2 cups / time 30 min

1 cup (125 g) pineapple finely chopped
2 tsp vegetable oil
1 tsp black mustard seeds
1/2 large red chili finely chopped or **1/2 tsp chili powder** *optional*
1/4 tsp black pepper ground
1/4 tsp coriander ground
2 tsp corn starch
1 Tbs lemon juice or **2 tsp rice vinegar**
2 tsp soy sauce (Shoyu)
1/2 cup (120 ml) water
3 Tbs sugar

1. Whisk **corn starch, lemon juice** (or **vinegar**), **soy sauce**, and **water** in a small bowl.
2. Heat **oil** in a small pot on medium high heat. Add **mustard seeds**. After they start to pop (20–30 sec), add **chili** (if using), ground **pepper**, and **coriander**. Fry 1 min, stirring constantly.
3. Stir in chopped **pineapple**. Fry, stirring constantly, until lightly braised, 2–3 min. Pour in whisked liquid. Add **sugar**. Bring to simmer and reduce heat to low.
4. Simmer and cook down to desired thickness, stirring regularly, 10–20 min. Allow to cool. Serve as dip for Batter-Fried Tofu Cubes (page 77) and other snacks, or with rice dishes.

Roasted Sesame Soy Sauce
nutty & tangy dip

makes about 1/3 cup / time 10 min

2 Tbs sesame seeds
1 Tbs soy sauce (Shoyu)
1 tsp coconut sugar or **agave syrup**
1 tsp rice vinegar or **coconut vinegar**
1–2 tsp water as needed

1. In a small pan, lightly roast **sesame seeds**. Allow to cool. Grind coarsely in a coffee grinder, small food processor, or mortar and pestle.
2. Transfer ground sesame to a small bowl. Mix in **soy sauce**, **coconut sugar** (or **agave syrup**), and **rice** (or **coconut**) **vinegar**.
3. Add some **water** gradually, if desired, to adjust sharpness and moderate taste.
4. Serve as dipping sauce or condiment for snacks and rice dishes, such as Nasi Kerabu (page 85).

Coconut Chutney
classic coconut condiment

makes about 1 cup / time 15 min +

1/2 cup (45 g) fresh coconut grated
or **1/3 cup (25 g) dried grated coconut + 2 Tbs hot water**
1 tsp vegetable oil
1 tsp black mustard seeds
1/4 tsp coriander ground
1/4 tsp cumin ground
1 tsp sugar or **agave syrup**
1 tsp lemon juice
1/2 tsp sea salt
3/4–1 cup (180 ml–240 ml) water

1. If using dried grated **coconut**, first mix well with hot water and soak 20 min.
2. Heat **oil** in a small frying pan on medium high heat. Add **mustard seeds**. After they start to pop (20–30 sec), add ground **coriander** and **cumin**. Fry 1 min, stirring constantly. Add grated **coconut**, **sugar**, **lemon juice**, and **salt**. Fry 2 min, stirring constantly. Remove from heat.
3. Transfer coconut spice mix to a small food processor. Adding **water** gradually, blend to desired texture. Adjust **lemon juice**, **salt**, and **sugar**, adding more as necessary to taste.
4. Allow to sit or chill for 1 hour. Serve with snacks, spicy dishes, and Roti Canai (page 113).

Chili Rice Sambal
simple spicy, crunchy condiment

makes about 1/3 cup / time 10 min +

2 Tbs brown rice (uncooked)
1 Tbs red chili flakes
1–2 tsp soy sauce (Shoyu)
1 tsp sesame oil

1. Heat a small frying pan on medium high heat. Lightly toast **brown rice**, mixing constantly, 3–5 min. Allow to cool. Grind coarsely with a small food processor or mortar and pestle.
2. Transfer ground brown rice to a small bowl. Add **red chili flakes** and 1 tsp each **soy sauce** and **sesame oil**. Mix well. Add more soy sauce to taste and for desired consistency.
3. Serve as a condiment or garnish for rice dishes, such as Nasi Kerabu (page 85).

黄闻铭
振慈
运程
合家平安
林水清
合家平安
宋喜良
财运

SOUPS

Penang Laksa
classic Malaysian noodle soup

serves 2 to 3 / time 45 min

5 oz (150 g) seitan sliced
3.5 oz (100 g) smoked tofu sliced
1/3 cup (45 g) pineapple chopped
1 Tbs vegetable oil
1 Tbs soy sauce or **Vegan Fish Sauce** (page 29)
7 oz (200 g) udon noodles (cooked)
2 1/2 cups (600 ml) water
2/3 cup (150 ml) coconut milk
1 kefir lime leaf or **1 tsp lime zest**
fresh mint leaves chopped
fresh coriander leaves chopped
fresh thai basil leaves chopped
bean sprouts for garnish

laksa spice paste:
4 candlenuts or **2 Tbs cashews** soaked 20 min in hot water, drained
1 stalk lemongrass chopped
1/2–1 large red chili chopped
2 cloves garlic chopped
1 shallot chopped
3/4 in (2 cm) fresh galangal or **ginger** chopped
1 tsp paprika ground
1/2 tsp fennel seed ground
1/2 tsp coriander ground
2 tsp coconut sugar or **agave syrup**
3/4 tsp sea salt
1 tsp tamarind paste (seedless)
2 Tbs lime juice or **lemon juice**
2 Tbs vegetable oil

1. If using dried Udon: Cook, rinse, and drain 3.5 oz (100 g) noodles according to package instructions.
2. Blend **spice paste ingredients** in a small food processor until smooth.
3. Heat 1 Tbs **oil** a large pot or wok on medium high heat. Add sliced **seitan** and **smoked tofu**. Fry, turning regularly until edges are browned and crispy, 3–5 min.
4. Stir in chopped **pineapple**. Continue to stir-fry, 2–3 min. Add **soy sauce** (or **Vegan Fish Sauce**). Fry 2–3 min. Transfer to a plate or bowl.
5. Return pot or wok to medium high heat. Fry blended spice paste until it darkens and oil starts to separate, stirring constantly, 3–5 min.
6. Gradually stir in **water**, **coconut milk** and **kefir lime leaf** (or **lime zest**). Bring to simmer. Add cooked **udon noodles**. Return to simmer. Cook until noodles have slightly softened, 3–5 min.
7. Stir in fried seitan, tofu, and pineapple. Turn off heat. Cover until ready to serve.
8. Portion soup and noodles into bowls. Garnish with chopped **herbs** and **bean sprouts**. Serve.

Curry Mee
traditional Nonya noodle soup

serves 2 to 3 / time 40 min +

7 oz (200 g) firm tofu cut in cubes
4.5 oz (125 g) mee noodles (thin wheat noodles)
1 Tbs vegetable oil
1/2 tsp coriander ground
1/4 tsp cumin ground
1/4 tsp black pepper ground
1/2 tsp paprika ground
1 Tbs soy sauce
2/3 cup (150 ml) coconut milk
10–15 fresh curry leaves
1 kefir lime leaf or **1 tsp lime zest** *optional*
1/2 large red chili finely sliced, for garnish
fresh coriander leaves chopped, for garnish

simple soup stock:

1/4 head small cabbage
1 large carrot chopped
1 bay leaf
1 star anise
2 1/2 cups (600 ml) water

spice paste:

4 candlenuts or **2 Tbs cashews** soaked in hot water 20 min, drained
1 stalk lemongrass chopped
1/2 large red chili chopped
2 cloves garlic chopped
1 shallot chopped
1 in (3 cm) fresh galangal or **ginger** chopped
1 tsp coconut sugar or **agave syrup**
3/4 tsp sea salt
1 Tbs lime juice or **lemon juice**
2 Tbs vegetable oil

1. Bring **stock ingredients** to boil in large pot. Reduce heat to low. Simmer 30 min. Strain, discard solids.
2. Blend **spice paste ingredients** in a small food processor until smooth.
3. Boil and drain **noodles** according to package instructions. Do not overcook.
4. Heat 1 Tbs **oil** in a large pot or wok on medium high heat. Add ground **coriander**, **cumin**, **pepper**, **paprika**, and **tofu cubes** and fry until golden brown, stirring regularly, 4–6 min.
5. Add **soy sauce** and blended **spice paste**. Mix well. Fry, stirring constantly, until richly aromatic and spice paste begins to darken, 5–7 min.
6. Stir in strained **soup stock**, **coconut milk**, **curry leaves**, and **kefir lime leaf** (or **zest**), if using. Bring to low boil. Reduce heat to low. Simmer, stirring regularly, 3–5 min. Add cooked **noodles**. Mix well. Remove from heat. Cover until ready to serve.
7. Garnish with sliced **red chili** and chopped fresh **coriander**. Serve.

Hokkien Mee

noodle soup with jackfruit, spinach & tofu

serves 3 to 4 / time 60 min +

3.5 oz (100 g) mee (wheat) noodles
3.5 oz (100 g) vermicelli (rice) noodles
7 oz (200 g) firm tofu
7 oz (200 g) green jackfruit chopped
3 cups (90 g) fresh spinach
1 cup (50 g) bean sprouts
2 shallots or **spring onions** finely chopped
3 cloves garlic chopped
1 in (3 cm) galangal or **ginger** finely chopped
1 stalk lemongrass finely chopped
1/2 large red chili finely chopped

4 cups (950 ml) Soup Stock (page 31)

2 Tbs vegetable oil + 1 Tbs vegetable oil
1 tsp coriander ground
1 tsp chili powder or **paprika** ground
1/2 tsp black pepper ground
1 Tbs peanut butter or **cashew butter**
3 Tbs Vegan Fish Sauce (page 29) or **soy sauce**
2 Tbs lime juice or **lemon juice**
1 Tbs brown sugar
1/2 tsp turmeric
3/4 tsp sea salt more as needed
1/4 tsp kala namak (black salt) *optional*

fresh coriander leaves chopped, for garnish
lime slices to serve

1. Cook or soak **mee noodles** and **vermicelli noodles** according to package instructions. Rinse in cold water. Drain and set aside.
2. Cut **tofu** in uniform slabs, wrap in clean kitchen towel. Weight with a heavy cutting board to press out excess moisture. Let sit 15 min. Unwrap tofu and crumble into a bowl.
3. Whisk 1 Tbs **peanut** (or **cashew**) **butter**, 3 Tbs **Vegan Fish Sauce** (or **soy sauce**), 2 Tbs **lime** (or **lemon**) **juice**, 1 Tbs **sugar**, and 1/2 tsp **salt** in a small bowl.
4. Heat 2 Tbs **oil** in a large frying pan or wok on medium high heat. Add chopped **shallots** (or **spring onions**), **garlic**, **galangal** (or **ginger**), **lemongrass**, **chili**, ground **coriander**, **chili powder** (or **paprika**), and **black pepper**. Fry until richly aromatic, stirring regularly, 2–3 min.
5. Add chopped **jackfruit**. Mix well. Fry, stirring frequently, until moderately scorched, 5–7 min. Stir in whisked sauce. Continue to fry until liquid is absorbed and jackfruit is deep reddish brown and scorched, another 4–5 min. Transfer spicy jackfruit to a bowl.
6. Heat 1 Tbs **oil** in frying pan or wok on medium high heat. Add crumbled **tofu**, **turmeric**, **kala namak** (if using), and 1/4 tsp **salt**. Mix well. Fry, stirring frequently, until tofu is lightly scorched and crispy, 3–5 min. Push tofu to the side and transfer jackfruit back to hot wok. Cover. Turn off heat.
7. Bring **soup stock** to simmer in a large pot. Add drained **mee** and **vermicelli noodles**, followed by **spinach** and **sprouts**. Stir a few times and turn off heat. Cover and let sit until spinach softens and shrinks, about 5 min.
8. Stir jackfruit and tofu into pot with broth and noodles before portioning everything into large bowls. Alternately, portion noodles and broth into bowls and top with spinach, sprouts, tofu, and jackfruit.
9. Serve with fresh chopped **coriander** and **lime slices**.

Variations:

One Wok Wonder: Make everything (with or without broth) in a single pot or wok. Simply stir-fry everything in the same order, slightly adjusting cooking times, spices and sauces, as needed.

Spicy Mushroom Noodle Soup
with crispy, crumbled tofu

serves 2 to 3 / time 45 min +

7 oz (200 g) firm tofu
4.5 oz (125 g) mee noodles (thin wheat noodles)
1 cup (100 g) mushrooms sliced or chopped
fresh coriander leaves chopped, for garnish
thai basil leaves chopped, for garnish
small handful enoki mushrooms for garnish
roasted onions for garnish

spice paste:

1 stalk lemongrass chopped
2 cloves garlic chopped
1 shallot or **spring onion** chopped
3/4 in (2 cm) galangal or **fresh ginger**
1 large red chili chopped *Optional*
3/4 in (2 cm) fresh turmeric
or **1/2 tsp turmeric powder**
2 tsp coconut sugar or **agave syrup**
3/4 tsp 5 Spice Powder (page 27)
1/2 tsp coriander ground
3 Tbs soy sauce (Shoyu)
1 Tbs rice vinegar
2 Tbs oil
1/2 tsp sea salt

soup stock:

2 dried shiitake mushrooms
2 carrots chopped
1 stalk celery chopped
or **1/2 small fennel bulb** chopped
2 bay leaves
5 cups (1200 ml) water

1. Bring **stock ingredients** to boil in large pot. Reduce heat to low. Simmer 30 min. Strain, discard solids.
2. Cut tofu in slabs, wrap in clean kitchen towel. Weight with heavy cutting boards to press out excess moisture. Let sit 15 min. Unwrap tofu and crumble into a bowl.
3. Blend **spice paste ingredients** in a small food processor until smooth. Use more oil if necessary.
4. Heat a medium frying pan on medium high heat. Stirring constantly, fry blended **spice paste** until it begins to darken and oil separates, 4–5 min. Reduce heat to low.
5. Remove 1/2 of fried **spice paste** and add to pot with (strained) **soup stock**. Stir well. Return stock to simmer on low heat.
6. Return pan with remaining spice paste to medium high heat. Add sliced **mushrooms** and crumbed **tofu**. Mix well. Frying, stirring regularly, until browned and crispy, 5–7 min. Remove from heat.
7. Add **noodles** to simmering soup stock. Cook on low, stirring occasionally, until noodles are soft, but not mushy, about 5 min.
8. Portion liquid and noodles into bowls. Top with fried **mushrooms** and **tofu**. Garnish with fresh **coriander** and **thai basil leaves**, **roasted onions**, and **enoki mushrooms**. Serve.

Wonton Soup
with vegetable & tofu dumplings

serves 3 to 4 / time 60 min +

3.5 oz (100 g) smoked tofu crumbled
3.5 oz (100 g) smoked tofu sliced thin
1 medium (90 g) carrot finely chopped, or grated
4–5 shiitake mushrooms finely chopped
6 cups (1400 ml) **Soup Stock** (page 31)

1 Tbs sesame oil
2 spring onions finely chopped
1/2 in (1 cm) fresh ginger finely chopped
1 clove garlic finely chopped
1/2 tsp coriander ground
3/4 tsp 5 Spice Powder (page 27)
2 tsp soy sauce (Shoyu)
2 tsp lemon juice
20–24 wonton wrappers

1. If using dried **shiitake mushrooms**, rinse and soak 10 min in hot water. Drain. Chop finely.
2. Chop **spring onions** and separate into white ends and greens. Save greens for garnish.
3. Heat **oil** in a frying pan on medium high heat. Add chopped **spring onions ends**, **ginger**, **garlic**, ground **coriander**, and **5 Spice Powder**. Fry 2 min, stirring constantly.
4. Add crumbled **tofu**, chopped or grated **carrot**, and chopped **mushrooms**. Mix well. Fry, stirring often, just until vegetables begin to soften, 3–5 min.
5. Add **soy sauce** and **lemon juice**. Mix well. Remove from heat.
6. Set up a small bowl with some water and **wonton wrappers** on a dry cutting board or counter surface. Put about 2 tsp of **filling** in the middle of a wonton wrapper. First, fold over two opposite corners to meet at the center and lightly press to seal using a few drops of water. Repeat with two other opposite corners. Press and seal wrapper around filling. Set aside. Continue making wontons until the filling is used up.
7. Bring (strained) **soup stock** to simmer on low heat. Carefully place filled, sealed wontons into broth. Watch that they do not stick to the bottom of the pot. Gently stir. After the wontons float up to the surface and are cooked, about 5 min, turn off the heat.
8. Portion liquid and 5 or 6 wontons into a bowl. Top with sliced **smoked tofu** and garnish with chopped **spring onion greens**. Serve.

Variations:
No Tofu: Substitute chopped seitan or vegetables (cabbage, carrot, zucchini, etc.) for tofu.

STARTERS & SIDES

Popiah
stuffed savory crêpes

makes 6 to 8 rolls / time 40 min +

1 cup (160 g) kohlrabi, jicama, or **turnip** peeled, grated
1 cup (100 g) Chinese cabbage (or regular/purple cabbage) finely chopped
1 large (100 g) carrot finely chopped
1 cup (100 g) green beans chopped

1 cup (140 g) flour (all purpose / type 550)
3 Tbs chickpea flour
4 Tbs flax seeds finely ground
3/4 tsp sea salt
1 3/4 cups (450 ml) water

4–6 Tbs Hoisin sauce
Sambal Belacan (page 50) or **chili sauce** (Srirachi)
1/3 cup (45 g) peanuts lightly roasted, crumbled
small bunch fresh mint leaves finely chopped

1. Combine **flour**, **chickpea flour**, ground **flax seeds**, and **salt** in a large mixing bowl. Stir in water and whisk until fairly thin and smooth, adding slightly more water if needed. Let sit 30 min.
2. Steam chopped **vegetables** in a bamboo steamer basket or large covered pot with 1/2 in (1 cm) water until blanched but still crisp, 4–6 min. Remove from heat.
3. Heat large frying pan on medium high heat. Put a few drops of **oil** on pan and rub it around with a paper towel. Do this before each crêpe, unless using a nonstick crêpe pan.
4. Pour 1/4 to 1/3 cup (60–80 ml) **batter** into middle of hot pan. Turn and tilt pan to form an evenly thin, circular crêpe about 8 in (20 cm) diameter. Cook until top surface is firm with small bubbles, 2–3 min. Lift edges and carefully flip with a spatula and cook another 1–2 min. Transfer crêpe to a plate and cover with a damp kitchen towel to keep soft. Continue for other crêpes.
5. Top a crêpe with steamed chopped **vegetables**, **Hoisin sauce**, **Sambal Belacan** (or **hot sauce**), crumbled **peanuts**, and chopped **mint leaves**. Roll one side up over filling, fold over ends, and roll tightly closed. Continue for others. Keep covered until ready to serve.

Variations:
Other Fillings: Substitute or add chopped kale, spinach, sweet potatoes, snow peas, sautéed (or steamed) seitan or smoked tofu, etc.

Otak-Otak
steamed spiced custard cakes

makes 8 to 10 pieces / time 50 min +

14 oz (400 g) tofu drained, crumbled
1/4 cup (30 g) cashews
2 Tbs vegetable oil
4 spring onions chopped
or **2 shallots** finely chopped
2 cloves garlic chopped
3/4 in (2 cm) fresh ginger chopped
3/4 in (2 cm) fresh turmeric chopped
or **1 tsp turmeric** ground
2 stalks lemongrass chopped
1 large green chili chopped *optional*
1/2 tsp cumin ground
1 tsp coriander ground
1/2 tsp black pepper ground

3/4 cup (180 ml) coconut milk
2 Tbs lime juice or **lemon juice**
1 Tbs soy sauce (Shoyu)
1 tsp tamarind paste (seedless)
1 Tbs corn starch
2 tsp agave syrup or **sugar**
1/4 tsp kala namak (black salt) *optional*
1/2 tsp sea salt

1 Nori (sushi) seaweed sheet crumbled
small bunch fresh curry leaves chopped
small bunch fresh thai basil leaves chopped
small bunch fresh mint leaves chopped
8–10 large banana leaves (e.g. frozen or fresh from Asian supermarket)
or **8–10 large kale** or (**savoy**) **cabbage leaves**

1. Soak **cashews** in hot water 20 min. Drain and discard water.
2. Heat 2 Tbs **oil** in a small frying pan on medium heat. Add chopped **onions**, **garlic**, **ginger**, **turmeric**, **lemongrass**, **chili**, ground **cumin**, **coriander**, and **pepper**. Fry, stirring constantly, 2–3 min. Turn off heat.
3. Crumble **tofu** into a blender. Add soaked **cashews**, **coconut milk**, **lime** (or **lemon**) **juice**, **soy sauce**, **tamarind**, **corn starch**, **agave syrup** (or **sugar**), **kala namak** (if using), and **salt**. Pulse a few times to chop. Add fried **spice paste**. Blend until smooth, stopping a few times to scrape down the sides. Transfer to large mixing bowl.
4. Add crumbled **nori seaweed**, fresh **curry**, **basil**, and mint leaves to blended tofu mix. Combine well.
5. Rinse and dry **banana leaves**. If using **kale** or **cabbage leaves**, soak in hot water 5 min to soften.
6. Spoon 3–4 Tbs of **filling** onto a flattened leaf. Fold opposite ends over and seal with a toothpick. Place in a steamer basket or pot with steamer tray and enough water. Steam until filling is firm, and a toothpick or knife comes out clean, 20–30 min.
7. Serve with Sambal Belacan (page 50), Sriracha or other hot sauce, or eat plain.

Variations:
Baked: Instead of steaming, bake in the oven at 425°F / 220°C / level 7 for 25–35 min.
Fruity: Blend filling also with 1/2 cup (75 g) chopped pineapple or ripe jackfruit.

Satay Skewers
with homemade seitan & peanut sauce

makes 6 to 8 pieces / time 40 min +

4 1/2 cups (1100 ml) Soup Stock (page 31) or **Simple Soup Stock** (page 63)
1 cup (135 g) vital wheat gluten flour (Seitan-Fix)
1 Tbs nutritional yeast flakes
1/2 tsp curry powder or **coriander** ground
1/2 tsp black pepper ground
1 tsp sugar
1/2 tsp sea salt
2 Tbs soy sauce
1 Tbs lemon juice
vegetable oil for frying

Batter:
3 Tbs rice flour
2 Tbs corn starch
1/2 tsp paprika
1/2 tsp thyme
1/2 tsp sea salt
1/4 (60 ml) water more as needed
1 Tbs soy sauce
1 Tbs lime juice

1. Bring 4 cups (975 ml) **Soup Stock** to boil in a medium pot. Reduce to low.
2. Combine **wheat gluten flour**, **nutritional yeast flakes**, **curry powder** (or **coriander**), **black pepper**, **sugar**, and **salt** in a large bowl. Add 1/2 cup (125 ml) **Soup Stock**, 2 Tbs **soy sauce**, and **lemon juice**. Mix well. Knead until smooth. Pull or cut into 12 to 16 pieces. Roll and form into thumb-sized chunks.
3. Simmer **seitan chunks** in broth 20 min. Remove and drain. Save broth for a soup, or discard.
4. Whisk **batter ingredients** into a thick, runny batter, adding slightly more water as needed.
5. Heat **oil** about 2 in (5 cm) deep in medium pot on medium high heat. Oil is hot enough when a drop of batter sizzles and comes to surface immediately.
6. Carefully slip **battered seitan pieces** into the hot oil. Fry until deep golden brown, 3–5 min, turning regularly with a slotted spoon. Do not crowd oil or the temperature will drop and they'll soak up oil instead of frying quickly. Wait 30–60 sec between batches for oil to heat back up. As pieces finish, drain and transfer to a plate with paper towels. Continue for all pieces.
7. Put fried chunks on skewers. Serve with Saus Kacang (page 51) or Simple Peanut Sauce (page 41).

Variations:
Store-bought Seitan: Use 10 oz (300 g) seitan, cut in chunks. **Mushrooms**: Replace seitan with oyster (or other) mushrooms. Batter and fry just like seitan. **Baked**: Instead of deep frying, bake battered, skewered pieces on a baking sheet at 425°F / 220°C / level 7 until golden brown, and crispy, 25–35 min.

Lemongrass Ginger Tofu
with grilled pineapple

serves 2 to 3 / time 25 min

14 oz (400 g) firm tofu cut in cubes or strips
1 1/2 cups (200 g) pineapple chopped
1 Tbs oil
2 shallots finely chopped
2 cloves garlic finely chopped
2 stalks lemongrass finely chopped
3/4 in (2 cm) fresh ginger finely chopped
1 tsp coriander ground
1 Tbs lime juice or **lemon juice**
1 Tbs soy sauce (Shoyu)
1/4 tsp sea salt
fresh coriander or **parsley leaves** chopped, for garnish

1. Cut **tofu** in slabs and wrap in clean kitchen towel. Weight with a heavy cutting board and press out extra moisture, 15–20 min. Unwrap and cut in cubes or strips.
2. Heat **oil** in a large frying pan or wok on medium high heat. Add chopped **shallots**, **garlic**, **lemongrass**, **ginger**, and ground **coriander**. Fry, stirring constantly, until shallots being to soften and brown, 2–3 min.
3. Add **tofu** cubes. Mix well. Fry, stirring regularly, until tofu cubes are golden brown and crispy on the edges, 5–8 min.
4. Add chopped **pineapple**, **lime** (or **lemon**) **juice**, **soy sauce**, and **salt**. Fry, stirring regularly, another 5–10 min. Remove from heat.
5. Garnish with chopped **coriander** or **parsley leaves** and serve.

Batter-fried Tofu Cubes
with Pineapple Pepper Chutney

serves 2 to 4 / time 30 min +

14 oz (400 g) firm tofu
3 Tbs rice flour
3 Tbs corn starch
2 Tbs lemon juice
1 Tbs soy sauce
1 Tbs water
vegetable oil for frying

1. Cut **tofu** in slabs, wrap in clean kitchen towel. Weight with a heavy cutting board and press out extra moisture 15–20 min. Unwrap and cut in cubes.
2. Combine **rice flour**, **corn starch**, **lemon juice**, **soy sauce**, and **water** in a large bowl.
3. Add **tofu** cubes. Combine well to coat thoroughly.
4. Heat **oil** about 2 in (5 cm) deep in medium pot on medium high heat. Oil is hot enough when a drop of batter sizzles and comes to surface immediately.
5. Carefully drop **battered tofu cubes** into the hot oil. Fry until deep golden brown, 3–5 min, turning regularly with a metal slotted spoon. Do not crowd oil or the temperature will drop and they'll soak up oil instead of frying quickly. Wait 30–60 sec between batches for oil to heat back up. As cubes finish frying, carefully drain and transfer to a plate or bowl with paper towels to absorb excess oil. Continue for all tofu cubes.
6. Serve with Pineapple Pepper Chutney (page 52) or Sambal Belacan (page 50).

Variations:

Baked: Instead of deep frying in oil, spread battered tofu cubes on a baking sheet or greased casserole dish and bake in a preheated oven at 425°F / 220°C / level 7 until deep golden brown, 25–35 min.

Spicy Tempeh Cubes
with curry leaves

serves 2 / time 20 min

7 oz (200 g) tempeh
20–30 fresh curry leaves or **small handful dried curry leaves**
2–3 Tbs vegetable oil
1 tsp chili powder or **paprika** ground
1/2 tsp turmeric ground
1 tsp sugar or **agave syrup**
1/2 tsp sea salt
2 tsp lemon juice or **lime juice**
lime slices for garnish

1. Cut **tempeh** in uniformly 3/4 in (2 cm) cubes.
2. Heat 2 Tbs **oil** in large frying pan or wok on medium high heat.
3. Add **tempeh cubes** and **curry leaves**. Fry, stirring frequently, 5–8 minutes until browned and oil is absorbed. Add **chili powder** (or ground **paprika**), **turmeric**, **sugar** (or **agave syrup**), **salt**, and **lemon** (or **lime**) **juice**. Continue to stir-fry, 3–5 min.
4. Serve with **lime slices**.

Variations:
Indian Twist: Add 1 tsp black mustard seeds, pinch asafoetida (hing) powder, and 1 tsp each ground cumin and coriander along with curry leaves. **Italian Fusion**: Add 1 Tbs tomato paste, 1 Tbs each fresh, chopped rosemary and thyme, 1 tsp balsamic vinegar, and 2 tsp soy sauce with spices.

Mushroom Murtabak
grilled stuffed flatbread

makes 4 pieces / time 45 min +

1 1/2 cups (200 g) flour (all purpose / type 550)
1/2 tsp sea salt
1/2 cup (120 ml) water
3 Tbs vegetable oil

1. Combine **flour** and **salt** in a large mixing bowl. Add **water** and 1 Tbs **oil**. Mix well. Knead to form a smooth, not-too-sticky dough, 2–3 min. If the dough is too sticky, add another 1–2 Tbs flour.
2. Add another Tbs of **oil** and continue to knead 2–3 min. Repeat this step with another Tbs **oil**. Knead several minutes until you have a soft, smooth, rubbery dough.
3. Separate dough into 4 balls. Lightly rub with **oil** and return to bowl. Cover bowl with plastic wrap. Let sit for minimum 2 hrs, ideally up 6 hrs in a warm place.

1 cup (100 g) mushrooms chopped
1/2 small red or **green bell pepper** chopped
or **1 medium tomato** chopped
2 spring onions finely chopped
1/2 in (1 cm) fresh ginger finely chopped
2 tsp vegetable oil
1/4 tsp coriander ground
1/4 tsp black pepper ground
1/4 tsp chili powder or **paprika** ground
1/4 tsp sea salt
1 tsp lemon juice or **lime juice** *optional*
1/2 tsp sugar *optional*

1. Heat **oil** in a medium frying pan on medium high heat. Add chopped **spring onions**, **ginger**, ground **coriander**, **black pepper**, **chili powder** (or **paprika**). Fry, stirring constantly until onions begin to brown and soften, 2–3 min.
2. Add chopped **mushrooms** and **bell pepper** (or **tomato**). Fry, stirring regularly, until mushrooms begin to soften, 4–5 min. Stir in salt. Remove from heat.
3. Roll out a dough ball as thin as possible on a clean, lightly greased flat surface. Put several tablespoons of filling in the middle of dough, spread filling, and fold over first two sides of dough, then the other sides. Press lightly down to seal. Continue for others.
4. Heat a large frying pan or crepe pan on medium heat. Fry stuffed flatbreads (without additional oil) until deep golden brown with brown spots, about 3–4 min per side.
5. Serve with curry, chutney, Sambal Belacan (page 50), or plain.

Variations:
Other Veg: Replace mushrooms with chopped zucchini, cauliflower, or sweet potato. **Seitan**: Replace mushrooms with sliced seitan. **Euro Twist**: Fry filling with chopped fresh thyme and rosemary.

Gobi 65
Indochinese spicy, crispy cauliflower

serves 2 to 4 / time 40 min

1/2 large head (450 g) cauliflower cut in small florets
3/4 in (2 cm) fresh ginger chopped
3–4 cloves garlic chopped
2 shallots chopped
2 large red chilies chopped
2 Tbs lemon juice
1 Tbs water
3 Tbs rice flour
2 Tbs chickpea flour
3 Tbs corn starch
1 tsp sugar
1 tsp chili powder or **paprika** ground
1 tsp coriander ground
10–12 curry leaves chopped or crumbled
1 tsp sea salt
vegetable oil for frying
cucumber slices for garnish
lime slices for garnish

1. Soak chopped **cauliflower** in hot water 5–10 min. Drain thoroughly, discard water.
2. Grind **ginger**, **garlic**, **shallots**, and **chilies** with **lemon juice** and 1 Tbs **water** in a small food processor until smooth.
3. Combine **rice flour**, **chickpea flour**, **corn starch**, **sugar**, **chili powder** (or **paprika**), **coriander**, **curry leaves**, and **salt** in a large mixing bowl.
4. Mix blended spice paste into dry ingredients. Add **cauliflower** pieces and mix well to coat thoroughly.
5. Heat **oil** about 2 in (5 cm) deep in medium pot on medium high heat. Oil is hot enough when a small piece of battered cauliflower sizzles and comes to surface almost immediately.
6. Carefully drop individual cauliflower pieces into the hot oil. Fry until deep golden brown, 3–5 min, turning regularly with a metal slotted spoon. Do not crowd oil or the temperature will drop and they'll soak up oil instead of frying quickly. Wait 30–60 sec between batches for oil to heat back up.
7. As pieces finish frying, carefully drain and transfer to a plate or bowl with paper towels to absorb excess oil. Continue for all pieces.
8. Serve with **cucumber** and **lime slices**.

Kangkung Goreng
stir-fried spinach with tofu & pineapple

serves 2 to 3 / time 25 min

5–6 cups (200 g) water spinach or **fresh spinach** chopped
7 oz (200 g) firm tofu cut in cubes or strips
1 cup (150 g) pineapple chopped
1 Tbs oil
2 cloves garlic finely chopped
1 red chili finely chopped *optional*
1/2 tsp coriander ground
1/4 tsp black pepper ground
1–2 Tbs soy sauce (Shoyu) or **Vegan Fish Sauce** (page 29)
1 Tbs lime juice or **lemon juice**
1 tsp sugar or **agave syrup**
1/4 tsp sea salt
fried onions for garnish

1. Heat **oil** in a large frying pan or wok on medium high heat. Add chopped **garlic**, red **chili** (if using), ground **coriander**, and **pepper**. Fry, stirring constantly, 1–2 min.
2. Add **tofu**, stir well. Fry, stirring constantly, until tofu is golden brown and lightly crispy, 5–7 min.
3. Mix in chopped **pineapple**, **soy sauce**, **lime** (or **lemon**) **juice**, and **agave syrup** (or **sugar**). Continue to stir-fry until pineapple is lightly braised, 3–4 min.
4. Add **spinach**. Mix well. Reduce heat to medium. Fry, partially covered, stirring regularly, until spinach shrinks and reaches desired softness, 2–5 min. Mix in **salt**. Remove from heat. Cover until ready to serve.
5. Garnish with **fried onions**. Serve with rice.

Braised Bok Choy
stir-fried Chinese cabbage

serves 2 / time 20 min

4 cups (300 g) bok choy chopped
1 small (70 g) tomato chopped
2 tsp oil
1/2 in (1 cm) fresh ginger finely sliced
1/4 tsp black pepper ground
1 Tbs soy sauce (Shoyu) or **Vegan Fish Sauce** (page 29)
1 Tbs water
1 tsp lemon juice
1 tsp coconut sugar or **agave syrup**
1/2 tsp corn starch
1/4 tsp sea salt

1. Whisk **soy sauce** (or **Vegan Fish Sauce**), **water**, **lemon juice**, **sugar** (or **agave syrup**), **corn starch**, and **salt** in a small bowl.
2. Heat **oil** in a large frying pan or wok on medium heat. Add sliced **ginger** and ground **pepper**. Fry, stirring constantly, until richly aromatic, 1–2 min.
3. Add chopped **bok choy**. Stir-fry, partially covered, until vegetable just starts to soften and leaves wilt, 2–3 min. Add chopped **tomato** and **soy sauce mix**. Stir well.
4. Continue to stir-fry, until vegetable is done (but still has some crunch) and sauce has thickened, another 2–3 min. Remove from heat.
5. Serve with rice.

Variations:
Smoked Tofu: Fry 3.5 oz (100 g) chopped smoked tofu for 2–3 minutes before adding bok choy.

Char Siu Bao
steamed buns with seitan filling

makes 6 to 8 pieces / time 45 min +

Bao steamed buns:

1 tsp active dry yeast
1 Tbs sugar
2/3 cup (160 ml) warm water
2 Tbs vegetable oil
2 cups (260 g) flour (all-purpose / type 550)
1 tsp baking powder
1/2 tsp sea salt

1. Whisk **dry yeast** and **sugar** with warm (not hot) **water** in a bowl. Let sit 5 min.
2. Combine **flour**, **baking powder**, and salt in a large mixing bowl. Mix in oil and water with yeast and sugar. Combine well with a fork or spatula and then knead 3–5 min with your hands to form a smooth, rubbery dough. Add slightly more flour if it is too sticky.
3. Separate dough into 6 to 8 equal pieces and roll to form a ball. Return to bowl. Cover and let sit in a warm place 2 hours, ideally up to 6–8 hrs.

Char Siu seitan filling:

10.5 oz (300 g) seitan finely chopped
1 medium carrot (80 g) finely chopped
1 Tbs vegetable oil
1 medium (80 g) red onion
or **2 spring onions** finely chopped
2 cloves garlic finely chopped
3/4 in (2 cm) fresh ginger finely chopped
1/2 tsp 5 Spice Powder (page 27)
or **1/2 tsp black pepper** ground
1 tsp coriander ground
1 tsp paprika ground
3 Tbs soy sauce (Shoyu)
1 Tbs rice vinegar
1 Tbs lemon juice
2 Tbs sugar
1/4 tsp sea salt
1 Tbs corn starch
1/4 cup (60 ml) water

1. Whisk **soy sauce**, **vinegar**, **lemon juice**, **sugar**, **salt**, **corn starch**, and **water** in a bowl until smooth.
2. Heat **oil** in a large frying pan or wok on medium high heat. Add chopped **onions**, **garlic**, **ginger**, **5 Spice Powder**, ground **coriander**, and **paprika**. Fry, stirring constantly, until onions start to soften, 2–3 min. Add chopped **carrots** and **seitan**. Continue to stir-fry until carrots begin to soften and seitan is moderately braised, 3–4 min. Pour in **soy sauce mix**. Mix well. Continue to fry until sauce thickens, 2–3 min. Remove from heat.
3. Bring 1 in (3 cm) water to boil in steamer pot with basket, or large pot with lid. Reduce to low simmer.
4. Flatten a dough ball on a lightly oiled surface (e.g. kitchen counter). Put about 2 Tbs of filling in the middle. Fold and pinch up edges, twisting and pressing together to close. Continue for other buns.
5. Place buns with at least a finger's width space and on baking paper in steamer basket or large pot with a plate at the bottom just above water level. Cover and steam until firm and springy, about 10–15 min. Depending on the size of steamer arrangement, you may need to steam 2 or 3 batches.

Variations:

Veg Mix: Omit seitan and make filling with 3 to 4 cups (350 g) chopped cabbage, mushrooms, zucchini, carrot, etc. **Tofu**: Replace seitan with firm tofu, cut into small cubes.

Pineapple Rice
golden, tangy & delicious

serves 2 to 3 / time 25 min

1 cup (190 g) jasmine or **basmati rice**
1/3 cup (45 g) pineapple finely chopped
1 Tbs vegetable oil
1 shallot finely chopped
1 clove garlic finely chopped
1/4 tsp black pepper ground
1/4 tsp coriander ground
1/2 tsp chili powder or **paprika** ground
1/2 tsp turmeric ground
1 pandan leaf or **bay leaf**
1/2 tsp sea salt
1 2/3 cup (400 ml) water

1. Rinse and drain **rice** well.
2. Heat **oil** in small pot on medium heat.
3. Add chopped **shallot**, **garlic**, ground **black pepper**, **coriander**, and **chili powder** (or **paprika**). Fry, stirring constantly, until shallots start to soften, 2–3 min.
4. Mix in **rice** and chopped **pineapple**, **turmeric**, **pandan** (or **bay leaf**) and **salt**. Fry, stirring constantly, 1–2 min.
5. While stirring, add **water**. Bring to low boil, reduce heat to low. Cover and simmer until liquid is mostly absorbed, 12–15 min.
6. Remove from heat. Mix several times gently with fork. Cover and let sit 5–10 min to absorb any remaining liquid.

MEALS &
MAIN DISHES

Nasi Lemak
Coconut Pandan Rice & Spicy Nuts

serves 4 / time 25 min

Coconut Pandan Rice:

2 cups (375 g) broken jasmine rice or **basmati rice**
1 2/3 cup (400 ml) water
1 2/3 cup (400 ml) coconut milk
1/2 tsp sea salt
1/2 tsp turmeric ground
2 pandan leaves or **bay leaves**
fried onions for **garnish**
1/2 small cucumber sliced
lime slices for garnish

1. Rinse and drain **rice** thoroughly.
2. Bring **water** and **coconut milk** to low boil in a medium pot with good lid. Stir in **rice**, **salt**, **turmeric**, and **pandan** (or **bay leaves**). Return to simmer. Cover and steam until most liquid is absorbed, 12–15 min. Remove from heat. Stir a few times. Cover and let sit 10 min. Remove and discard leaves before serving.
3. Garnish with **fried onions**, **cucumber**, and **lime slices**.
4. Serve with Lemongrass Ginger Tofu (page 75), Sambal Belacan (page 50), and Spicy Nuts (below).

Spicy Nuts:

1/2 cup (50 g) peanuts
1/2 cup (50 g) cashews
1/2 tsp chili powder or **paprika** ground
2 tsp coconut sugar
1/4 tsp sea salt

1. Heat a medium frying pan on medium heat. Dry roast **peanuts** and **cashews**, stirring regularly, until light golden brown and dark spots begin to appear, 4–7 min. Do not burn.
2. Add **chili powder** (or **paprika**), **sugar** and **salt**. Mix well. Continue to cook another 2–3 min, stirring constantly, until sugar has melted and nuts are well coated. Remove from heat. Allow to cool.

Nasi Kandar
with KLFC – Kuala Lumpur Fried Chicken

serves 2 to 3 / time 45 min

10.5 oz (300 g) seitan sliced or chopped
vegetable oil for frying

dry mix:
1/3 cup (40 g) flour (all purpose / type 550)
1/3 cup (40 g) rice flour
1/2 tsp baking powder
1/2 tsp paprika ground
1/2 tsp thyme
1/2 tsp black pepper ground
1 tsp sea salt

wet mix:
2 Tbs corn starch
1 Tbs nutritional yeast flakes
1 Tbs soy sauce
2 Tbs lemon juice
1–2 Tbs water as needed
1 clove garlic finely chopped
1 shallot finely chopped
1/2 large red chili finely chopped

1. Combine **dry mix ingredients** in large bowl. Whisk **wet mix ingredients** in another large bowl, adding **water** last and as needed.
2. Toss **seitan** chunks in dry mix until well coated. Mix floured seitan chunks in the bowl with wet mix. Toss wet pieces in dry mix again, coating all sides.
3. Heat **oil** about 2 in (5 cm) deep in medium pot on medium high heat. Test the temperature of the oil by carefully slipping a small battered piece into the hot oil. It should sizzle immediately and float to the surface within 30 sec.
4. Fry 7 to 10 pieces at a time. Do not overcrowd oil. Turn pieces to fry evenly deep golden brown, 3–5 min. Remove with a slotted spoon, dripping excess oil back into pot. Transfer to a plate lined with paper towels. Continue until all pieces are done.
5. Serve KLFC with Sambal Belacan (page 50) or other hot sauce, hoisin sauce, ketchup, etc. For Nasi Kandar meal, serve with Pineapple Rice (page 90) and Aubergine & Okra Curry (page 117).

Nasi Kerabu
mix-it-yourself rice & salad

serves 3 to 4 / time 30 min

Mushroom Olive Rice:

1 cup (190 g) broken jasmine rice or **short grain brown rice**
1 2/3 cup (400 ml) water
1/2 tsp sea salt
3/4 cup (80 g) mushrooms finely chopped
1/2 cup (50 g) black olives finely chopped
1 Tbs olive oil or **vegetable oil**
1/4 tsp black pepper ground
1/4 tsp coriander ground
2 tsp lemon juice or **lime juice**

1. Rinse and drain **rice**.
2. Bring **water** and **salt** to boil in a medium pot with lid. Stir in rice. Return to bowl. Reduce to low. Cover and simmer until rice has absorbed most of liquid, 12–15 min (longer if using brown rice). Remove from heat.
3. Heat **oil** in a medium frying pan on medium heat. Add ground **pepper**, **coriander**, chopped **mushrooms**, and **olives**. Fry just until mushrooms begin to soften, 3–5 min. Remove from heat. Stir in **lemon** (or **lime**) **juice**.
4. After rice is cooked, carefully but thoroughly mix in lightly fried mushrooms and olives. Cover and let sit 10 min before serving.

Four Greens:

small handful fresh parsley greens
small handful fresh coriander greens
small handful fresh thai basil leaves
small handful fresh mint leaves

Grated Beet, Carrot & Radish:

1 medium beet peeled, grated
1 medium carrot peeled, grated
1 cup (100 g) radish (e.g. daikon) grated
3 tsp lemon juice
1/4 tsp sea salt *optional*

1. Rinse, drain, dry all **greens** thoroughly. Finely chop and combine together in a bowl.
2. Grate **beet**, **carrot**, and **radish** separately into small bowls. Add 1 tsp **lemon juice** and a pinch of salt to each, if desired. Toss.
3. Serve Mushroom Olive Rice with Four Greens, Grated Beet, Carrot, and Radish, with Serunding Kelapa (page 49), Roasted Sesame Soy Sauce (page 52), and Chili Rice Sambal (page 53).

Nasi Goreng
traditional vegetable fried rice

serves 2 to 3 / time 40 min +

3.5 oz (100 g) firm tofu
1 cup (190 g) broken jasmine rice or **short grain brown rice**
1/2 tsp sea salt
1 2/3 cup (400 ml) water
1 cup (100 g) chinese cabbage, cauliflower, broccoli or **bok choy** finely chopped
1 medium (90 g) carrot finely chopped or sliced
2–3 Tbs oil
1 tsp sesame oil *optional*
3 (50 g) spring onions chopped, separated into white ends and greens
1–2 cloves garlic finely chopped
1 large red chili finely chopped *optional*
1/2 in. (1 cm) fresh galangal or **ginger** finely chopped
1 tsp coriander ground
1/2 tsp black pepper ground
2 Tbs soy sauce (Shoyu)
1 Tbs lime juice or **lemon juice** or **2 tsp rice vinegar**
1 tsp lime zest or **lemon zest** *optional*
1 tsp sugar or **agave syrup**
1/2 tsp sea salt
lime slices for garnish

1. Cut **tofu** in slabs, wrap in clean kitchen towel. Weight with heavy cutting boards to press out excess moisture. Let sit 20 min. Unwrap tofu and crumble into a bowl.
2. Wash and drain **rice** thoroughly.
3. Bring **water** to boil in a small pot. Add **rice** and **salt**. Stir. Return to boil. Reduce heat to low and cover. Simmer 12 to 20 min as needed. After water is absorbed, remove from heat. Fluff rice with a fork. Cover and let sit and cool, ideally an hour or more.
4. Heat **oil** in a large wok or frying pan on medium high. Add chopped **spring onion ends**, **garlic**, **chili** (if using), **galangal** (or **ginger**), ground **coriander**, and **black pepper**. Fry, stirring constantly, until lightly browned, 2–3 min.
5. Add chopped **carrots**. Fry, stirring constantly, 2–3 min. Add crumbled **tofu**. Mix well. Fry, stirring regularly, until tofu begins to turn golden brown, 3–5 min. Add chopped **cabbage** (or other **vegetables**). Fry, stirring constantly, until vegetables start to soften, 4–5 min.
6. Whisk **soy sauce**, **lime** (or **lemon**) **juice**, **zest**, **sugar** (or **agave syrup**), and **sea salt** in a small bowl.
7. Add cooked **rice** to frying **vegetables**. Mix well. Add **soy sauce mix** and **spring onions greens**. Combine well. Fry, stirring constantly until liquid has been absorbed and rice and vegetables are moderately browned, 5–7 min. Remove from heat. Cover until ready to serve.
8. Serve with **lime slices**.

Mee Goreng
traditional vegetable fried noodles

serves 2 / time 30 min

4.5 oz (125 g) mee noodles (thin wheat noodles)
1 cup (100 g) cabbage or **broccoli** finely chopped
1 medium carrot (90 g) finely chopped or sliced
2–3 Tbs vegetable oil
2 spring onions or **shallots** finely chopped
1–2 cloves garlic finely chopped
1/2 in (1 cm) fresh galangal or **ginger** finely chopped
1 large red chili finely chopped *optional*
1 tsp coriander ground
1/2 tsp black pepper ground
2 Tbs soy sauce (Shoyu)
1 Tbs lime juice or **lemon juice**
or **2 tsp rice vinegar**
1 tsp tamarind paste (seedless)
2 tsp agave syrup or **sugar**
1/2 tsp sea salt
fresh coriander leaves chopped, for garnish
lime slices to serve

1. Cook or soak **mee noodles** according to package instructions. Drain, cover, set aside.
2. Whisk **soy sauce**, **lime** (or **lemon**) **juice** (or **vinegar**), **tamarind**, **agave syrup** (or sugar), and **salt** in a small bowl.
3. Heat **oil** in a large frying pan or wok on medium high heat. Add chopped **spring onions ends** (or **shallots**), **garlic**, **galangal** (or **ginger**), **chili**, ground **coriander**, and **pepper**. Fry, stirring constantly, until onions begin to soften, 3–4 min.
4. Add **carrots** and **cabbage** (or **broccoli**). Stir-fry until vegetables soften and brown, 4–6 min.
5. Add cooked, drained **noodles**. Mix well. Pour in **soy sauce mix**. Continue to cook, stirring frequently, until vegetables are cooked and noodles lightly braised, 3–5 min. Remove from heat. Stir in **spring onion greens**. Cover until ready to serve.
6. Garnish with fresh chopped **coriander**. Serve with **lime slices**.

Variations:
Tofu or Seitan: Fry 3.5 oz (100 g) sliced seitan strips or crumbled firm tofu along with vegetables. Increase soy sauce to 3 Tbs. **Mushrooms**: Add 1/2 cup (50 g) sliced or chopped mushrooms. **Go Nuts**: Garnish with roasted, crumbled peanuts or cashews. **Thicker Sauce**: Whisk in 2 Tbs water and 1 tsp corn starch with other soy sauce ingredients.

Assam Pedas
baked tamarind tofu-fish

serves 3 to 4 / time 50 min +

14 oz (400 g) firm tofu
2/3 cup (100 g) pineapple finely chopped
4 bean curd sheets (tofu skins)
4 roasted seaweed (nori) sheets (for sushi)
2 Tbs vegetable oil more as needed
2 shallots or spring onions finely chopped
2 cloves garlic finely chopped
3/4 in (2 cm) galangal or **ginger** finely chopped
2 stalks lemongrass finely chopped
1 large red chili finely chopped *optional*
2 large bay leaves
1/2 tsp turmeric ground
1 tsp coriander ground
1/2 tsp paprika ground
1/2 tsp black pepper ground
1/4 tsp sea salt

2 Tbs soy sauce (Shoyu)
2 tsp tamarind paste (seedless)
2 Tbs agave syrup or **brown rice syrup**
2 Tbs lime juice or **lemon juice**
1 Tbs rice vinegar
1 tsp corn starch

small bunch fresh thai basil leaves chopped
fresh parsley leaves chopped, for garnish
lime slices for garnish

1. Soak **bean curd sheets** in hot water until soft and rubbery, about 15 min.
2. Cut **tofu** in slabs, wrap in clean kitchen towel. Weight with a heavy cutting board and press out extra moisture for 15 min. Unwrap and crumble into a bowl.
3. Heat 2 Tbs **oil** in a large frying pan or wok on medium high heat. Add chopped **shallots** (or **spring onions**), **garlic**, **galangal** (or **ginger**), **chili** (if using), **bay leaves**, ground **turmeric**, **coriander**, **paprika**, and **black pepper**. Fry, stirring constantly, until richly aromatic, 2–3 min.
4. Mix in crumbled **tofu** and chopped **pineapple**. Fry, stirring regularly, until tofu is golden brown and lightly scorched, 5–7 min. Remove from heat. Remove and discard **bay leaves**. Combine chopped **thai basil leaves** and **salt** with fried tofu and spices.
5. Whisk **soy sauce**, **tamarind paste**, **agave** (or **brown rice**) **syrup**, **lime** (or **lemon**) **juice**, **rice vinegar**, and **corn starch** in a small bowl.
6. Preheat oven to 425°F / 220°C / level 7. Grease a large, glass casserole dish with **oil**. Alternately, use a large nonstick bake form.
7. Drain soaked **bean curd sheet** and lay flat on cutting board or clean surface. Place a **seaweed sheet** on top of bean curd sheet. Spoon 1/4th of cooked **tofu filling** across middle of seaweed sheet. Fold one side of sheets up over filling. Roll firmly closed with open ends. Place in glass dish or bake form. Repeat for others and pack snugly together. Pour **soy tamarind sauce** evenly over rolls.
8. Bake until surface is deep golden brown and crispy, filling is firm, and liquid is mostly absorbed, about 30–40 min, turning dish half way through to bake evenly. Remove from oven. Let sit 10 min.
9. Garnish with fresh chopped **parsley** and **lime slices**. Serve with rice.

Variations:
Tomato: Substitute 1 Tbs tomato paste for tamarind paste.

Sayur Campur
stir-fried mixed vegetables

serves 2 to 3 / time 25 min

4 cups (250 g) Chinese broccoli, bok choy, or **cabbage** chopped
1 medium (100 g) carrot sliced or chopped
1 medium tomato chopped
2 Tbs vegetable oil
2 spring onions or **shallots** finely chopped
2 cloves garlic finely chopped
3/4 in (2 cm) fresh galangal or **ginger** finely chopped
1/2 stalk lemongrass chopped
1/2 tsp coriander ground
1/4 tsp black pepper ground
3 Tbs soy sauce (Shoyu) or **Vegan Fish Sauce** (page 29)
1 Tbs rice vinegar
2 tsp coconut sugar or **brown sugar**
1/4 cup (60 ml) water
1 Tbs corn starch
1/4–1/2 tsp sea salt
fried onions for garnish

1. Whisk **soy sauce** (or **Vegan Fish Sauce**), **rice vinegar**, **sugar**, **water**, **corn starch**, and **salt** in bowl.
2. Heat **oil** in a large frying pan or wok on medium high heat. Add chopped **onions** (or **shallots**), **garlic**, **galangal** (or **ginger**), **lemongrass**, ground **coriander**, and **pepper**. Fry, stirring constantly, until richly aromatic and onions begin to soften, 2–3 min.
3. Add chopped **broccoli** (or other **vegetables**) and **carrots**. Mix well. Fry, partially covered, stirring regularly, until vegetables begin to soften, 4–7 min.
4. Add chopped **tomato** and stir in soy sauce mix. Reduce heat to medium. Stir-fry until vegetables are done and sauce has thickened, 3–5 min. Remove from heat. Cover until ready to serve.
5. Garnish with **fried onions** and serve with rice.

Variations:
Other Veg: Substitute any other combination of vegetables. **Fruity**: Add 1 cup (125 g) fresh chopped pineapple along with vegetables.

Sayur Lodeh
mixed vegetables with creamy coconut sauce

serves 2 to 3 / time 35 min

1 cup (90 g) cabbage chopped
1 cup (90 g) green beans chopped
1 cup (90 g) snow peas chopped
1 medium (80 g) carrot chopped
1 medium (80 g) tomato chopped
1 cup (240 ml) coconut milk
fried onions for garnish

spice paste:

3 candlenuts or **2 Tbs cashews**
2 shallots or **1 medium red onion** chopped
2 cloves garlic chopped
1 stalk lemongrass chopped
1/2 in (1 cm) fresh galangal or **ginger** finely chopped
1/2 in (1 cm) fresh turmeric peeled, chopped or **1/2 tsp turmeric** ground
1 tsp coriander ground
1/2 tsp black pepper ground
1 Tbs lime juice
1 tsp coconut sugar
3/4 tsp sea salt
2 Tbs vegetable oil

1. Soak **candlenuts** or **cashews** in hot water 20 min. Drain and discard water.
2. Grind **spice paste ingredients** in a small food processor until smooth.
3. Heat a large frying pan or wok on medium heat. Fry spice paste, stirring constantly, until it darkens and oil begins to separate, 3–5 min.
4. Add chopped **vegetables**. Mix well with spice paste. Fry, stirring frequently, until vegetables begin to braise and soften, 5–8 min.
5. Stir in **coconut milk**. Bring to simmer. Reduce heat to low. Continue to cook, partially covered, stirring occasionally, until vegetables are desired consistency, another 5–10 min. Stir in some water while simmering for a thinner, lighter sauce. Adjust **salt** to taste.
6. Garnish with **fried onions** and serve with rice.

Variations:

Other Veg: Substitute or add chopped bamboo shoots, eggplant, cauliflower, broccoli, etc. Adjust soy sauce and salt as needed.

Soya Rendang

spicy coconut curry

serves 2 to 3 / time 45 min

2 cups (125 g) large soy chunks (TVP)
1 1/4 cups (300 ml) water or **Soup Stock** (page 31)
1/2 cup (50 g) fresh coconut grated
or **1/3 cup (25 g) dried grated coconut + 3 Tbs hot water**
1 stalk lemongrass chopped
2 cloves garlic chopped
2 shallots chopped
1–2 large red chilies chopped
3 Tbs oil
1/2 cup (120 ml) coconut milk
1/2 tsp black pepper ground
1 tsp coriander ground
1 tsp cumin ground
1/2 tsp fennel ground
1 tsp paprika ground
1 tsp turmeric ground
small handful curry leaves or **3 bay leaves**
1 medium (90 g) tomato chopped
1 Tbs lime juice or **lemon juice**
1 Tbs sugar or **agave syrup**
1 tsp sea salt

1. Bring 1 1/4 cup (300 ml) **water** (or **Soup Stock**) to boil in a medium pot. Stir in **soy chunks**. Cover. Remove from heat. Let sit 10–15 min.
2. If using **dried grated coconut**, combine well with hot water and let sit 10 min.
3. Blend chopped **lemongrass**, **garlic**, **shallot**, **chilies**, and 3 Tbs **oil** in a small food processor until smooth. Use slightly more oil if necessary.
4. Heat a large frying pan or wok on medium high heat. Add ground **pepper**, **coriander**, **cumin**, **fennel**, **paprika**, and **turmeric**. Dry roast until fragrant, 1–2 min. Stir in blended **spice paste**. Fry until paste darkens and oil begins to separate, 4–5 min.
5. Drain soaked soy chunks. Press out any remaining liquid. Add **soy chunks** and **curry leaves** (or **bay leaves**) to frying spice paste. Combine well. Fry, stirring frequently, 5–7 min.
6. Add grated **coconut**, chopped **tomato**, **lime** (or **lemon**) **juice**, and **sugar** (or **agave syrup**). Stir well. Fry, stirring frequently, 3–5 min.
7. Stir in **coconut milk**. Bring to simmer, reduce heat to low. Add **salt**. Simmer, partially covered, stirring regularly, until liquid is mostly absorbed, 5–10 min. Remove from heat.
8. Keep covered until ready to serve. Serve with rice or flatbread (e.g. roti).

Variations:

Seitan: Substitute 10 oz (300 g) chopped seitan for soaked soy chunks.

Banana Leaf Meal
featuring South Indian Sweet Potato Dal

serves 3 to 4 / time 30 min

1 large (180 g) sweet potato chopped
1 cup (185 g) red lentils
2 cups (480 ml) water more as needed
1 Tbs vegetable oil
1 tsp black mustard seeds
1 shallot finely chopped
1 clove garlic finely chopped
1/2 in (1 cm) fresh ginger finely chopped
1 tsp cumin ground
1/2 tsp coriander ground
8–10 curry leaves or **1 bay leaf**
1/2 cinnamon stick or **1/2 tsp cinnamon** ground
1 tsp turmeric ground
2 Tbs lime juice or **lemon juice**
1 tsp agave syrup or **sugar**
1 tsp sea salt
1 cup (240 ml) coconut milk
or **3/4 cup (180 ml) water + 3 Tbs coconut cream**

1. Rinse and drain **lentils**. Bring 2 cups **water** to boil in a medium pot. Stir in lentils. Bring to boil. Reduce heat to medium low and cook, adding **water** if needed, stirring occasionally, until lentils are soft, 12–20 min. Turn off heat.
2. Heat **oil** in a large pot on medium high heat. Add **mustard seeds**. After they start to pop (20–30 sec), add chopped **shallot**, **garlic**, **ginger**, ground **cumin**, **coriander**, and **curry leaves** (or **bay leaf**). Fry, stirring constantly, until shallots start to soften, 2–3 min.
3. Add chopped **sweet potato**. Mix well. Fry, stirring regularly, until potato starts to soften, 5–8 min.
4. Pour in cooked **lentils**. Add **cinnamon**, **turmeric**, **lime** (or **lemon**) **juice**, **agave syrup** (or **sugar**), and **salt**. Mix well. Bring to simmer. Stir in **coconut milk** gradually. Reduce heat to low. Continue to simmer to desired thickness, another 5–15 min. Adjust **salt** and **lime juice** to taste.
5. Serve with rice, papadam, and other curries, vegetable dishes, and salads, such as Shredded Beet Salad (page 37) and Urap (page 47) or Acar (page 45).

Variations:
Vedic: Omit shallot and garlic. Replace with a pinch asafoetida (hing) powder, if desired.

Roti Canai
grilled flatbread with curry & chutney

makes 4 pieces / time 30 min +

1 1/2 cups (200 g) flour (all purpose / type 550)
1/2 tsp sea salt
1/2 cup (120 ml) water
3–4 Tbs vegetable oil more as needed

1. Combine **flour** and **salt** in a large mixing bowl. Add **water** and 1 Tbs **oil**. Mix well and knead to form a smooth, not-too-sticky dough, 2–3 min. If the dough is too sticky, add another 1–2 Tbs flour.
2. Add another Tbs of **oil** and continue to knead 2–3 min. Repeat this step with another 1–2 Tbs **oil**. Knead several minutes until you have a soft, smooth, rubbery dough.
3. Separate dough into 4 balls. Lightly rub with **oil** and return to bowl. Cover bowl with plastic wrap. Let sit for minimum 2 hrs, ideally up 6 hrs in a warm place.
4. Uncover and briefly knead each ball. Let sit 5 min while you prepare the clean, flat surface (e.g. counter) by thinly greasing with vegetable oil.
5. Rub some oil on your hands and flatten a dough ball on the oiled surface. Press, spread, or roll as thin as possible, flipping several times. Fold each side in on itself towards the middle and repeat with the top and bottom. Lightly press flat. Set aside and repeat with other balls.
6. Heat a large, flat pan on medium high heat. If not using nonstick or well-seasoned cookware, first rub a few drops of **oil** on the surface of the pan with a paper towel.
7. Fry each roti until golden brown with dark spots, about 2–4 min each side. Wrap in clean, damp kitchen towels to keep warm and soft until ready to serve.
8. Serve with Red Curry (page 115) and Coconut Chutney (page 53).

Red Curry
with tofu, potato, pineapple & peanuts

serves 2 to 3 / time 40 min

7 oz (200 g) firm tofu cut in cubes
10–12 small (250 g) new potatoes chopped
1 medium red onion chopped
1/2 cup (45 g) peanuts or **cashews** lightly roasted, crumbled
1 1/2 cups (180 g) pineapple chopped
1 medium (80 g) tomato chopped
10–12 curry leaves
1 Tbs lime juice or **lemon juice**
1 cup (240 ml) coconut milk
1/2 cup (120 ml) water if desired
3/4 tsp sea salt
fresh coriander leaves chopped, for garnish

red curry spice paste:

2–3 Tbs vegetable oil
1 shallot finely chopped
1 clove garlic finely chopped
3/4 in (2 cm) fresh ginger finely chopped
1 large red chili chopped *optional*
1 stalk lemongrass finely chopped
1/2 tsp coriander ground
1/2 tsp black pepper ground
1/2 tsp turmeric ground
1 tsp chili powder or **paprika** ground

1. Grind **spice paste ingredients** until smooth in a small food processor or mortar and pestle.
2. Heat a large pot or wok on medium heat. Fry spice paste, stirring constantly, until it darkens and oil begins to separate, 4–6 min.
3. Add chopped **tofu**, **potatoes**, and **onion**. Mix well. Fry, partially covered, stirring frequently, until tofu starts to brown on edges and potatoes begin to soften, 5–7 min.
4. Add **peanuts** (or **cashews**), chopped **pineapple**, **tomato**, **curry leaves**, and **lime** (or **lemon juice**). Mix well. Fry 1–2 min.
5. Gradually stir in **coconut milk**. Bring to simmer. Reduce heat to low. Cook, stirring regularly, until potatoes are soft, adding some **water** if desired for a thinner curry, 6–10 min.
6. Add **salt**. Mix well. Remove from heat. Keep covered until ready to serve.
7. Garnish with fresh chopped **coriander leaves** and more crumbled **nuts**.
Serve with Roti Canai (page 113) or rice.

Aubergine & Okra
quickie curry

serves 2 to 3 / time 25 min

1 medium (250 g) eggplant chopped
1 medium (90 g) tomato chopped
3 cups (250 g) okra
2–3 Tbs vegetable oil
1 small onion chopped
1 clove garlic finely chopped
3/4 in (2 cm) fresh ginger finely chopped
1/2 tsp coriander ground
1/4 tsp black pepper
1 Tbs soy sauce (Shoyu)
1 Tbs lemon juice or **2 tsp rice vinegar**
1 tsp sugar or **agave syrup**
1/2 tsp sea salt
fresh coriander or **parsley** chopped, for garnish

1. Rinse, drain, and dry **okra** well. Cut and discard okra tips and ends. Slice remaining okra into equal sized pieces.
2. Heat **oil** in a large frying pan or wok on medium high heat. Add chopped **onion**, **garlic**, **ginger**, ground **coriander**, and **pepper**. Fry, stirring constantly until onions begin to soften, 3–4 min.
3. Add chopped **eggplant**. Mix well. Fry 5 min, stirring regularly.
4. Add sliced **okra**. Fry 3–5 min, stirring regularly.
5. Whisk **soy sauce**, **lemon juice** (or **vinegar**), **sugar** (or **agave syrup**), and **salt** in a small bowl. Add, along with **tomato**, to okra and eggplant. Mix well. Continue to fry on medium heat, partially covered, stirring occasionally, 5–7 min.
6. Top with chopped **coriander** or **parsley**. Serve with rice or roti.

Punjabi Sizzler
cashew tomato curry with seitan

serves 2 / time 30 min

7 oz (200 g) seitan chopped
3 medium (200 g) tomatoes chopped
1/3 cup (45 g) cashews
1 cup (240 ml) water
2 Tbs vegetable oil
1 medium red onion or **2 shallots** chopped
2 cloves garlic chopped
1 large red chili chopped
3/4 in (2 cm) fresh ginger chopped
1 tsp black mustard seeds
1 tsp cumin ground
1 tsp coriander ground
1/2 tsp fenugreek seeds ground
1/2 tsp garam masala ground
1/4 tsp cinnamon ground
1/2 tsp turmeric ground
2 bay leaves
8–10 curry leaves
2 Tbs lime juice or **lemon juice**
1 Tbs sugar
1 tsp sea salt
fresh coriander leaves chopped, for garnish

1. Soak **cashews** several hours (or overnight) in water. Drain and discard water.
2. Blend chopped **tomatoes** and soaked **cashews** with 1 cup (240 ml) fresh **water** in a food processor or high-power blender until smooth, adding water last and gradually.
3. Heat 2 Tbs **oil** in a large frying pan or wok on medium high heat. Add **mustard seeds.** After they start to pop (20–30 sec), add ground **cumin**, **coriander**, **fenugreek**, **garam masala**, **cinnamon**, and **turmeric**. Stir several times. Add chopped **onion** (or **shallots**), **garlic**, **chili**, and **ginger**. Fry, stirring constantly, until richly aromatic, 2–3 min.
4. Mix in chopped **seitan**, **bay leaves**, and **curry leaves**. Fry, partially covered, stirring regularly, until lightly braised, 2–4 min.
5. Add blended **cashews** and **tomatoes**. Stir well. Bring to simmer and reduce heat to low. Simmer, stirring frequently, partially covered, until sauce darkens and thickens, 10–15 min. Mix in **lime** (or **lemon**) **juice**, **sugar**, and **salt**. Remove from heat. Keep covered until ready to serve.
6. Garnish with **coriander leaves** and serve with rice or roti, or other flatbread.

Variations:
Fruity: Add 3/4 cup (90 g) chopped pineapple or mango and 2 Tbs raisins along with seitan. **Tofu**: Replace seitan with regular or smoked tofu. **Veg Chicken**: Use sliced, vegan chicken nuggets or cutlets instead of seitan.

Mushroom Manchurian
Indochinese dumplings in gravy

serves 2 to 3 / time 40 min

Manchurian dumplings:

5–8 medium (160 g) mushrooms finely chopped
1 cup (110 g) cabbage finely chopped
3/4 cup (100 g) flour (all-purpose / type 550)
1/4 tsp turmeric ground
1/2 tsp ajwan seeds or **thyme**
1/2 tsp sea salt
1/3–1/2 cup (80–120 ml) water
vegetable oil for frying

1. Combine all **dumpling ingredients** (except oil) in a large mixing bowl. Add **water** last and gradually, mixing with a fork, to create sticky batter. Use more water or flour as necessary.
2. Heat **oil** about 2 in (5 cm) deep in medium pot on medium high heat. Oil is hot enough when a small drop of batter sizzles and comes to surface immediately.
3. Wet hands and form walnut sized balls. Carefully drop balls into hot oil using a spoon. Fry 5 or 6 dumplings at a time until deep golden brown, 3–5 min, turning occasionally. As pieces finish frying, carefully drain and transfer to a plate or bowl. Repeat for all dumplings.

gravy:

2 medium (160 g) tomatoes chopped
1 medium red onion or **2 spring onions** finely chopped
3/4 in (2 cm) fresh ginger finely chopped
2 cloves garlic
1 Tbs vegetable oil
1/2 tsp black mustard seeds
1/2 tsp black pepper ground
1/2 tsp chili powder or **paprika** ground
1/2 tsp coriander ground
3 Tbs soy sauce (Shoyu)
1 Tbs lemon juice
1 Tbs sugar
1 Tbs corn starch
2/3 cup (160 ml) water
fresh coriander or **parsley leaves** chopped, for garnish

1. Whisk **soy sauce**, **lemon juice**, **sugar**, **corn starch**, and **water** in a bowl.
2. Heat 1 Tbs **oil** in a medium pot or frying pan on medium heat. Add **mustard seeds.** After they start to pop (20–30 sec), stir in chopped **onion**, **ginger**, **garlic**, **pepper**, **chili powder** (or paprika) and **coriander**. Fry until onions begin to soften, stirring constantly, 3–4 min.
3. Stir in **whisked liquid**. Add chopped **tomatoes**. Bring to simmer. Reduce heat to low. Simmer, stirring regularly, until sauce thickens, 3–5 min. Add **fried dumplings** and mix well. Cook, partially covered, 2–3 min. Turn off heat. Cover until ready to serve.
4. Garnish with fresh, chopped **coriander** or **parsley** and serve with rice or flatbread.

Black Pepper Seitan & Broccoli
stir-fried superstar

serves 2 to 3 / time 30 min

7 oz (200 g) seitan chopped
3 cups (250 g) broccoli chopped in small florets
1 medium (100 g) red onion chopped
2 cloves garlic finely chopped
3/4 in (2 cm) fresh ginger finely chopped

1 Tbs lime juice
1 Tbs soy sauce (Shoyu)
1 tsp agave syrup or **sugar**
2 Tbs water
1 tsp corn starch
1/2 tsp sea salt
2 Tbs vegetable oil
3/4 tsp black pepper ground
3/4 tsp coriander ground
small handful chives finely chopped, for garnish

1. Whisk **lime juice**, **soy sauce**, **agave syrup** (or **sugar**), **water**, **corn starch**, and **salt** in a small bowl.
2. Heat oil in a large frying pan or wok on medium high heat. Add chopped **onion**, **garlic**, **ginger**, ground **black pepper**, and **coriander**. Fry, stirring constantly, until onions begin to soften.
3. Add chopped **seitan** and **broccoli**. Mix well. Fry, stirring regularly, until seitan is braised and broccoli begins to soften, 5–7 min.
4. Stir in **soy sauce mix**. Mix well. Continue to fry, mixing regularly, until vegetables are done and sauce has thickened, 3–5 min.
5. Garnish with chopped **chives**. Serve with rice.

Variations:
Fruity: Add 1 cup (120 g) chopped pineapple or mango. **Redder**: Add 1 Tbs tomato paste and 1 chopped tomato along with soy sauce mix. Adjust salt as needed.

Szechuan Seitan
batter-fried & spicy

serves 2 to 4 / time 45 min +

1/2 cup (65 g) flour (all purpose / type 550)
1/4 cup (30 g) rice flour
1 Tbs corn starch
3/4 tsp baking powder
1/2 tsp sea salt
3/4 cup (180 ml) water as needed
vegetable oil for frying

7 oz (200 g) seitan chopped or sliced
2 cups (180 g) broccoli chopped in small florets
3/4 cup (100 g) pineapple chopped
1 small (70 g) red pepper chopped

1. Combine **flour**, **rice flour**, **corn starch**, **baking powder**, and **salt** in a large mixing bowl. Gradually stir in **water** to form a smooth, thick batter. Cover and let sit 20 min.
2. Heat **oil** about 2 in (5 cm) deep in medium pot on medium high heat. Oil is hot enough when a drop of batter sizzles and comes to surface immediately.
3. Add **seitan** pieces to batter and mix well.
4. Carefully slip battered seitan pieces into the hot oil. Fry until deep golden brown, 3–5 min, turning regularly with a metal slotted spoon. Do not crowd oil or the temperature will drop and they'll soak up oil instead of frying quickly. Wait 30–60 sec between batches for oil to heat back up.
5. As pieces finish frying, carefully drain and transfer to a plate or bowl with paper towels to absorb excess oil. Continue for all pieces.

1 Tbs sesame oil
2 spring onions chopped
2 cloves garlic finely chopped
1 in (3 cm) fresh ginger finely chopped
1–2 red chilies finely chopped
1/2–1 tsp Szechuan pepper ground
1/2 tsp coriander ground

3 Tbs soy sauce (Shoyu)
2 Tbs rice vinegar
3 Tbs sugar
2 Tbs corn starch
1 tsp lemon zest
3/4 cup (180 ml) water
2 Tbs cashews lightly roasted, crumbled

1. Whisk **soy sauce**, **vinegar**, **sugar**, **corn starch**, **lemon zest**, and **water** in a small bowl.
2. Heat **sesame oil** in a large pot or wok on medium heat. Add chopped **spring onions, garlic, ginger, chilies**, ground **pepper**, and **coriander**. Fry, stirring constantly, until onions soften, 3–4 min.
3. Add chopped **broccoli** and **pineapple**. Mix well. Fry, stirring regularly, until broccoli begins to soften, 4–5 min. Mix in chopped **red pepper**. Fry another 2–3 min.
4. Pour in whisked sauce and stir well. Simmer, stirring regularly, until vegetables are desired softness, another 2–5 min. Carefully stir in batter-fried seitan pieces. Mix well. Cover. Turn off heat.
5. Garnish with crumbled **cashews** and serve.

Variations:
Szechuan Gobi: Use chopped cauliflower instead of seitan.

Char Kuey Teow
stir-fried flat rice noodles

serves 3 to 4 / time 30 min +

7 oz (200 g) seitan chopped or sliced
7 oz (200 g) firm tofu
7 oz (200 g) thick, flat rice noodles
2 Tbs vegetable oil
2 shallots finely chopped
2 cloves garlic finely chopped
3/4 in (2 cm) fresh ginger finely chopped
1/2 tsp black pepper ground
2 Tbs soy sauce (Shoyu)
1 Tbs kecap manis (sweet soy sauce)
or **1 Tbs soy sauce + 1 tsp sugar**
1 Tbs lime juice or **lemon juice**
2 Tbs water
1 tsp corn starch
5–8 fresh thai basil leaves for garnish
small handful fresh scallions finely chopped, for garnish
bean sprouts for garnish
lime slices for garnish

1. Soak **rice noodles** in warm water 20–30 min (according to package instructions).
2. Cut **tofu** in slabs, wrap in a clean kitchen towel, and place weight (e.g. heavy cutting board) on top to press out extra moisture. After 20 min, unwrap and crumble into a bowl.
3. In a small bowl, whisk **soy sauce**, **kecap manis** (or more **soy sauce** + 1 tsp **sugar**), **lime** (or **lemon**) **juice**, 2 Tbs water, and 1 tsp corn starch.
4. Heat **oil** in a large frying pan or wok on medium high heat. Add chopped **shallots**, **garlic**, **ginger**, and **black pepper**. Fry, stirring constantly, until shallots begin to soften, 2–3 min.
5. Add chopped **seitan** and **tofu**. Mix well. Fry, stirring frequently, until seitan and tofu being to scorch and get crispy, 4–6 min.
6. Drain soaked **noodles** and add to frying pan. Mix well several times. Pour in **soy sauce** mixture. Continue to stir-fry, mixing often, until sauce thickens and noodles are desired texture, another 5–7 min. Remove from heat and cover until ready to serve.
7. Garnish with fresh **basil leaves**, **scallions**, and **bean sprouts** before serving. Alternately, mix in toppings for final minute of stir-frying. Serve with **lime slices**.

Variations:
Go Nuts: Top with 2–3 Tbs roasted, crumbled cashews or peanuts.

Hong Shao Rou
roasted jackfruit

serves 2 / time 45 min +

2 1/2 cups (350 g) green jackfruit (unsweetened) chopped
2 shallots or spring onions chopped
2–3 cloves garlic finely chopped
3/4 in (2 cm) fresh ginger finely chopped
2 Tbs vegetable oil
1 tsp coriander ground
1/2 tsp black pepper
1 1/2 tsp paprika ground
2 Tbs lemon or **lime juice**
or **1 Tbs rice vinegar**
1 Tbs coconut sugar or **sugar**
3/4 tsp sea salt
fresh coriander or **parsley** chopped, for garnish

1. If using canned **jackfruit**, discard liquid, rinse and drain jackfruit well before chopping. Pieces should be fairly small and thin (but not finely chopped).
2. Combine **all ingredients** (except fresh coriander or parsley) well in a large bowl and marinate 2 hrs (or overnight in the fridge), stirring once or twice.
3. Preheat oven to 425°F / 220°C / level 7.
4. Mix ingredients once more and evenly spread marinated jackfruit into a glass bakeware dish or nonstick metal baking tray. Pour any remaining marinade over jackfruit.
5. Bake for 20 min then briefly remove from oven to mix, mash and turn mixture. Return to oven and continue to bake until jackfruit is a deep reddish brown and scorched and crispy outside, but still tender and juicy inside, another 15–25 min.
6. Garnish with chopped **coriander** or **parsley**. Serve with rice or roti (e.g. flatbread).

Variations:
Pan-Fried: Instead of baking, cook jackfruit mixture, partially covered in a wok or large pot on medium high heat, stirring frequently, until liquid is absorbed and jackfruit is deep reddish brown and scorched, 12–20 min. **Vedic**: Omit shallots (or onions) and garlic. Add 1/2 tsp ground cumin, 1/4 tsp asafoetida (hing) powder, and 1 tsp thyme.

Ran

DESSERTS & DRINKS

Cendol
iced coconut milk, green noodles & syrup

serves 2 / time 30 min +

5 fresh pandan leaves
1 2/3 cup (400 ml) water
1/2 cup (60 g) rice flour
1 Tbs sugar
1/4 tsp sea salt
20 ice cubes
1 cup (240 ml) coconut milk
2 Tbs palm syrup or **agave syrup**
fresh berries for garnish

1. Blend chopped **pandan leaves** with **water** in a small food processor or blender. Pour through a strainer into a bowl and press lightly on pulp to extract juice. Discard green pulp.
2. Whisk **rice flour**, **sugar**, **salt**, and strained green juice in a medium pot. Bring to simmer and reduce to low heat. Stirring constantly, cook until mixtures begins to thicken, about 10 min.
3. Let noodle batter cool, 10–15 min. Set up a bowl of ice water with about 2 cups cold water and 8–10 **ice cubes**.
4. Fill an icing bag with the cooled batter mixture. Using a round (ca. 1 mm) tip, squeeze out (short or long) noodles into ice water. Let sit to solidify.
5. Blend 10–12 **ice cubes** in a blender. Scoop blended ice into 2 chilled glasses or bowls. Drizzle 1 Tbs palm syrup (or agave syrup) over the ice in each glass.
6. Drain noodles well. Arrange in glasses.
7. Pour about 1/2 cup (120 ml) **coconut milk** into each glass.
8. Garnish with fresh **berries** and serve.

Variations:
Matcha: Omit pandan. Whisk 1 tsp cooking matcha powder into 1 1/2 cups (375 ml) water.

Ais Kacang

coconut ice cream, jackfruit & pandan syrup

serves 2 to 3 / time 30 min +

coconut ice cream:

1 2/3 cup (400 ml) coconut milk (min. 60%)
3 Tbs sugar
1/2 tsp locust bean gum *optional*

1 1/2 cups (150 g) yellow jackfruit (sweet) chopped

green pandan syrup:

5 pandan leaves chopped
1/2 cup (95 g) sugar
1/2 tsp agar powder or **corn starch**
2/3 cup (160 ml) water

1. Blend **coconut milk** with **sugar**, and **locust bean gum** in a blender until smooth, 60–90 sec. Pour into 2 ice cube trays or several small bowls and freeze 6 hours or overnight.
2. Blend chopped **pandan leaves** with **water** in a small food processor or blender. Pour through a strainer into a bowl and press lightly on pulp to extract juice. Discard green pulp.
3. Combine 1/4 cup (60 ml) of **green pandan juice**, 1/2 cup (95 g) **sugar**, and 1/2 tsp **agar powder** (or **corn starch**) in a small pot. Simmer gently on low heat, stirring occasionally, until sugar is dissolved, about 5 min. Remove from heat. Allow to cool and thicken.
4. Blend frozen **coconut milk mix** in a high-powered blender, using the tamper and more coconut milk or some of the remaining green pandan juice as needed to create a smooth, thick ice cream. Stop occasionally to scrape down the sides. If ice cream is melting and too runny, transfer to a large bowl and freeze for 30–60 min before serving.
5. Scoop **ice cream** into chilled bowls. Top with chopped **jackfruit** and **green pandan syrup** and serve.

Variations:

Other Fruit: Add or substitute chopped mango or pineapple for jackfruit. **Simple Syrup**: Skip the pandan syrup and if desired, top with agave, palm, or brown rice syrup instead.

Kueh Dadar
green crêpes with sweet coconut filling

makes 6 to 8 crêpes / time 45 min +

coconut filling:

2 cups (180 g) fresh coconut grated
or **1 cup (85 g) dried grated coconut + 1/2 cup (120 ml) hot water**
1/2 cup (65 g) brown sugar or **coconut sugar**

1. If using **dried grated coconut**, first mix well with hot **water** and soak 20 min.
2. Heat a small frying pan or pot on medium low heat. Add grated **coconut** and **sugar**. Mix well. Cook 3–5 min, partially covered, stirring frequently, until sugar has melted. If needed, add 1–2 tsp water. Turn off heat. Leave covered until crêpes are ready.

crêpes:

1 cup (125 g) flour (all-purpose / type 550)
1 Tbs chickpea flour
1 Tbs corn starch
1/2 tsp baking powder
2 Tbs sugar
1/4 tsp sea salt
1/3 cup (80 ml) soy milk
2 tsp oil
4 pandan leaves chopped
1 cup (240 ml) water more as needed

1. Combine **flour**, **chickpea flour**, **corn starch**, **baking powder**, **sugar**, and **salt** in a large mixing bowl.
2. Blend chopped **pandan leaves** with 1 cup (240 ml) **water** in a small food processor or blender. Pour through a strainer into a bowl and press lightly on pulp to extract juice. Discard green pulp.
3. Whisk **soy milk** (or **coconut milk**) and **oil** with **green pandan water**.
4. Whisk wet ingredients into dry to form a mostly, smooth batter, adding 1–2 Tbs more **water** if needed. Do not over mix. Cover and let batter sit 20–30 min.
5. Heat frying pan on medium high heat. When a drop of water sizzles and dances of the surface of the pan, it's ready. Pour enough batter onto pan to form a large, evenly thin crêpe, lifting and tilting the pan to let the batter run.
6. Cook until several bubbles form on crêpe, 2–3 min. Lift up edges first, then flip carefully with spatula and press down lightly. Cook 1–2 min on other side. Transfer to a plate and cover to keep warm. Continue for all crêpes.
7. Put 2–3 Tbs coconut filling on a crêpe. Roll one edge and then fold both ends in toward the middle. Roll closed. Continue for all.

Variations:

Banana Berry: Instead of coconut filling, just use chopped bananas and berries.
Matcha: Omit pandan. Instead, whisk 1 tsp cooking matcha powder into 3/4 cup (180 ml) water.

Kueh Lapis
traditional multi-color cake

makes 8 to 10 slices / time 60 min +

1 1/2 cups (185 g) flour
1 cup (195 g) sugar
2 Tbs chickpea flour
1 Tbs corn starch
1 1/2 tsp baking powder
1 tsp vanilla sugar or **extract**
1/2 tsp cinnamon ground
1/4 tsp cardamom ground
1/4 tsp sea salt

2/3 cup (150 g) margarine (e.g. Earth Balance or Alsan)
or **coconut oil** (extra virgin)
1/2 cup (120 ml) soy milk
1 tsp rice vinegar
4 pandan leaves or **1 tsp cooking matcha powder**
1 medium beet peeled, chopped
1 in (3 cm) fresh turmeric peeled, chopped or **3/4 tsp turmeric** ground
2 cups (500 ml) water

1. Grind **sugar** in a food processor or dry container of a high-powered blender until fine, 30–60 sec.
2. Combine all **dry ingredients** in a large mixing bowl. Separate into three equal portions and put in three medium bowls or large measuring cups, ideally with a pouring spout.
3. Whisk **soy milk** and **rice vinegar** in a small bowl or glass until it thickens, 30 sec.
4. Heat **margarine** (or **coconut oil**) gently in pot on low heat until melted. Stir in **soy milk** and **vinegar**.
5. Pour warm liquid mix equally into each of the medium bowls (or measuring cups) with dry mix. It should be slightly more than 1/3 cup (85 ml) each. Stir each to create a thick, mostly smooth batter.
6. Blend **pandan leaves** (or **matcha powder**), **beet**, and **turmeric** separately with approximately 2/3 cup (150 ml) water each, rinsing the blender out after each. Strain each colored water into its own small bowl or glass, discarding solids.
7. Measure 1/3 cup (80 ml) of each **colored water** and add to each batter to create a green, red, and yellow batter. The batter should be fairly thin, runny, and smooth. Whisk in slightly more **colored water** if needed.
8. Preheat oven to 425°F / 220°C / level 7. Lightly grease a small, narrow, rectangular metal loaf pan (e.g. 4 x 12 in / 10 x 30 cm) with **oil**.
9. Pour 1/2 of the green batter evenly into the pan to fill pan and form the first layer. Put on the top rack of the oven. Bake until the surface is firm, 5–10 min. Remove from oven. Pour 1/2 of the yellow batter evenly over the green layer. Return to the oven. Bake until surface of this layer is firm, 4–6 min. Remove from the oven. Pour 1/2 of the red batter over the yellow layer. Return to oven and bake another 4–6 min. Repeat for another green, yellow, and red layer, baking for 4–6 min each.
10. Reduce oven temperature to 375°F / 190°C / level 5. Return pan to oven on middle rack. Bake until a toothpick comes out clean, about 10 min. Remove from oven. Allow to cool 30 min.
11. Carefully loosen edges with a knife or spatula and turn cake onto a cutting board. Slice and serve.

Ondeh-Ondeh
steamed rice dumplings with syrup filling

makes 18 to 24 pieces / time 40 min +

1 cup (105 g) glutinous rice flour
3 Tbs sugar
1/4 tsp sea salt
4 pandan leaves chopped
2/3 cup (150 ml) water
1/3 cup (60 g) brown sugar
1/2 cup (45 g) dried grated coconut
1/4 cup (60 ml) hot water

1. Combine dried grated **coconut** with 1/4 cup (60 ml) **hot water**. Soak 20 min.
2. Blend chopped **pandan leaves** with 2/3 cup (150 ml) **water** in a small food processor or blender. Pour through a strainer into a bowl and press lightly on pulp to extract juice. Discard green pulp.
3. Combine **rice flour**, 3 Tbs **sugar**, and **salt** in a mixing bowl. Stir in about 1/2 cup (120 ml) strained **green juice** and mix well to create a smooth, rubbery dough. Use slightly more juice as needed.
4. Bring a medium pot of water to rapid boil on medium high heat.
5. Using about 1 Tbs of dough, roll a ball and then press it flat. Put 1/2 tsp **brown sugar** in the center and carefully press the dumpling closed.
6. Drop the dumplings directly into the boiling water, watching that they do not stick to the bottom of the pot. Boil 5 to 6 dumplings at a time until they float to the surface, 3–4 min.
7. Carefully remove with a slotted spoon. Drain. Roll boiled dumplings in soaked coconut flakes and transfer to a plate. Continue for all.

Variations:
No Pandan: Make white dumplings using just water instead of the blended green pandan juice.
Matcha Green: Whisk 1 tsp cooking matcha powder into 1/2 cup (120 ml) water for green liquid.
Fruit-filled: Instead of sugar, fill dumplings with a raspberry, chopped strawberries, etc. Adjust sweetness of dough accordingly.

Apam Balik

crispy, crunchy peanut-filled pancakes

makes 4 to 6 / time 30 min +

3/4 cup (100 g) peanuts crumbled or very coarsely ground
2 Tbs sugar
1/4 tsp sea salt
1/2 cup (60 g) flour (all purpose / type 550)
1/2 cup (50 g) rice flour
1/4 cup (45 g) sugar
1 Tbs corn starch
1 tsp baking powder
1/2 tsp sea salt
1 cup (240 ml) coconut milk
2 Tbs water
agave syrup or **palm syrup** *optional*
vegetable oil for frying pan

1. Crumble or coarsely grind **peanuts** and dry roast in a pan on medium heat until golden brown and dark spots appear, 4–5 min. Add **sugar** and **salt**. Mix well. Stirring constantly, roast until sugar melts and mix starts to stick together, 1–2 min. Remove from heat.
2. Combine **flour**, **rice flour**, **sugar**, **corn starch**, **baking powder**, and **salt** in a large mixing bowl. Whisk in **coconut milk** and **water** gradually. Mix until mostly smooth, but do not over mix. Cover and let batter sit 20–30 min.
3. Heat frying pan on medium high heat. Put a few drops of **oil** on pan and rub it around with a paper towel. Do this before each pancake. When a drop of water sizzles and dances on surface, pan is ready.
4. Pour about 1/4 to 1/3 cup (60–80 ml) batter in the center of the hot pan. Tilt and turn the pan to form a large, thin, circular pancake.
5. After bubbles appear on surface and underside is golden brown (about 2–3 min), use a spatula to carefully peel up the edges around the pancake and then flip it over. Cook the other side for 1–2 min, then flip it back over. Put 2–3 Tbs of the sugary **peanuts** on the pancake and roll up or fold over. Transfer to a plate. Repeat with other pancakes.
6. Serve plain, or drizzle pancakes with **agave syrup** or **palm syrup**.

Variations:

Creamy: Use peanut butter instead of roasted, crumbled peanuts. **Bananas**: Add sliced banana to filling. **Traditional**: Add 1–2 Tbs sweet corn kernels to each each pancake filling.

Kuih Kodok
traditional banana fritters

makes about 20 pieces / time 35 min +

1 large (150 g) ripe banana chopped
1/3 cup (80 ml) coconut milk
1 tsp rice vinegar
1/3 cup (40 g) rice flour
1/2 tsp cinnamon ground
2 Tbs sugar
1/4 tsp vanilla bean ground
1/2 tsp baking powder
2 tsp corn starch
1/4 tsp sea salt
vegetable oil for frying

1. Whisk **coconut milk** and **vinegar** in a small bowl.
2. Combine **rice flour**, **cinnamon**, **sugar**, **vanilla**, **baking powder**, **corn starch**, and **salt** in a large mixing bowl.
3. Gradually stir **coconut milk** into flour mix to create a smooth, thick batter using as much liquid as needed. Add slightly more **coconut milk** if needed. Add chopped **bananas** and combine well. Let sit 20 min.
4. Heat **oil** about 2 in (5 cm) deep in medium pot on medium high heat. Oil is hot enough when a small piece of batter sizzles and comes to surface immediately.
5. Carefully slide about 1 Tbs of battered banana mix into the hot oil. Fry until deep golden brown, 3–5 min, turning regularly with a metal slotted spoon. Do not crowd oil or the temperature will drop and they'll soak up oil instead of frying quickly. Wait 30–60 sec between batches for oil to heat back up.
6. As pieces finish frying, carefully drain and transfer to a plate lined with paper towels to absorb excess oil. Continue for all pieces.

Lychee Banana Sorbet
frozen tropical fruity dessert

serves 2 / time 20 min +

2 medium (250 g) bananas
1 cup / 7 oz (200 g) lychees peeled
1–2 Tbs soy milk or **rice milk**
fresh mint leaves chopped, for garnish
1/4 cup (30 g) walnuts lightly roasted, crumbled

1. If using canned **lychees**, drain syrup.
2. Peel and chop **bananas**. Along with drained **lychees**, freeze in a closed container or freezer bag 8 hrs or overnight. Also chill 2 bowls in the freezer, if desired.
3. Blend frozen, chopped **bananas** and **lychees** with 1–2 Tbs **soy** (or **rice**) **milk** in a high-powered blender, using the tamper and more **milk** (or **lychee syrup**) as needed to create a smooth sorbet. Stop occasionally to scrape down the sides. Don't run the blender too long or too high or the sorbet will melt. (If sorbet is melted, chill in the freezer for 30 min.)
4. Scoop into (chilled) bowls. Garnish with fresh chopped **mint leaves** and crumbled **walnuts**. Serve and eat immediately.

Variations:
Fruitier: Instead of soy milk or rice milk, alternately blend with 1–2 Tbs of lychee syrup.

Cold White Coffee
blended, frosty treat

serves 2 / time 20 min +

1/2 cup (120 ml) espresso or **strong coffee**
1/4 cup (35 g) cashew pieces
1 cup (240 ml) cold water
10–12 ice cubes
1/2 tsp vanilla bean ground
1–2 Tbs sugar

1. Make **espresso** (or **coffee**) and allow to cool.
2. Soak **cashews** in hot water 15 min. Rinse in cold water. Drain.
3. Blend **espresso** (or **coffee**), soaked **cashews**, **cold water**, **ice cubes**, **vanilla**, and **sugar** in a blender until smooth, 1–2 min.
4. Pour into chilled glasses and enjoy.

Variations:
Cocoa: Blend with 2–3 tsp cacao nibs or cocoa powder. **Chai-Style**: Blend with 1/2 in (1 cm) fresh ginger and 1/4 tsp each: ground cardamom, cloves, and nutmeg. Adjust sugar as desired, or substitute with 2 or 3 chopped dates.

Lemon Iced Tea
classic refresher

serves 2 / time 15 min +

2 Tbs loose black tea or **2 bags black tea** (e.g. Assam, Darjeeling, Ceylon)
2 1/2 cups (600 ml) water
8–12 ice cubes
2 Tbs lemon juice or **lime juice**
1–2 Tbs sugar or **agave syrup**
fresh mint leaves

1. Chill 2 large glasses in the freezer for 1 hr or more.
2. Put 1 1/4 cup (300 ml) **water** in a glass in the fridge to chill.
3. Bring 1 1/4 cup (300 ml) **water** to simmer in a medium pot. Turn off heat. Let cool 2–3 min.
4. Steep **tea** in **hot water** until strongly brewed, 6–8 min. Strain and discard tea leaves, or remove and discard tea bags. Let brewed tea sit and cool 30 min.
5. Stir **sugar** (or **agave syrup**) into tea until dissolved. Stir in **lemon juice** and cold **water**.
6. Put some **mint leaves** and several **ice cubes** in each chilled glass.
   Add lemon tea and stir a few times. Serve.

Variations:

Green Tea: Simply replace black tea with green tea. **Lemongrass & Ginger**: Steep tea along with 1 stalk chopped lemongrass and 1/2 in (1 cm) fresh ginger.

Apple Cucumber Juice
cooling delicious

serves 2 / time 15 min +

3 medium apples chopped
1 large (200 g) cucumber peeled, chopped
2 1/2 cups (600 ml) cold water
4–8 ice cubes

1. Chill 2 large glasses in the freezer for 1 hr or more.
2. Chill **apples**, **cucumber**, and **water** for 2 hrs or more in fridge.
3. Blend **all ingredients** in a blender until smooth, 45–60 sec.
4. Strain (if desired) and pour into chilled glasses.

Variations:
Extra Fresh: Add a small handful of fresh mint leaves, and 1/2 in (1 cm) fresh chopped ginger.
Juicer: Instead of blending, run chopped apples and cucumber through a juicer. Pour into chilled glasses. Add cold water and ice cubes if desired.

Ginger Lime Soda
iced, refreshing & energizing

serves 2 / time 10 min +

3/4 in (2 cm) fresh ginger chopped
2 Tbs lime juice or **lemon juice**
2 cups (480 ml) cold sparkling water
8–12 ice cubes
2–3 Tbs agave syrup or **sugar**
lime slices for garnish

1. Chill 2 large glasses in the freezer for 1 hr or more.
2. Blend **all ingredients** in a blender. Adjust sweetness to taste.
3. Pour into chilled glasses. Garnish with a **lime slice** and serve.

Variations:
Peach Fizzy: Blend with 1 chopped peach. **Orange**: Add or substitute 1 cup (240 ml) fresh squeezed orange juice for lime (or lemon) juice, reduce or omit agave syrup (or sugar) if desired. **Berry**: Add a handful of frozen raspberries or strawberries.

Purple Dream
chilled apple, beet & pineapple delight

serves 2 / time 15 min +

2 medium apples chopped
2 medium beets peeled, chopped
1 1/2 cups (200 g) pineapple chopped
2 cups (480 ml) cold water
4–6 ice cubes

1. Chill 2 large glasses in the freezer for 1 hr or more.
2. Chill **apples**, **beets**, and **pineapple** for 2 hrs or more in fridge.
3. Blend **all ingredients** in a blender until smooth, 45–60 sec.
4. Strain (if desired) and pour into chilled glasses.

Variations:
Berry: Add a small handful of frozen strawberries or raspberries. **Juicer**: Instead of blending, run chilled, chopped beets, apples, pineapple through a juicer. Pour into chilled glasses. Add some cold water and ice cubes, if desired.

PTE LTD
50 Buffalo Road
219799
63417741
62911658

for **Kolja Govinda**

Thanks for inspiration, love & support
Julia, Mom, Dad, Adam, Spencer, Ian

Jens Neumann & Oliver Schmitt – Ventil Verlag
Joachim & Uschi – Kochen ohne Knochen & Ox Fanzine
Bernd Drosihn, Surdham Göb, Nicole Just
Claudia Renner, Jérôme Eckmeier, Sebastian Copien,
Björn Moschinski, Marc Pierschel, Stefanie Witt
Terry Hope Romero, Christoph Rupprecht
Sarah Kaufmann – Vegan Guerilla
Monika Kanokova – Kickstarter
Kirstin Knufmann – Pure Raw
Simon Beck – Govinda Natur
Jule & Micha – Chaostheorie
Jan Bredack – Veganz
Thomas Reichel – Avesu
Dirk Bocklage – Vegan River Cruises
Sascha C. Schalthöfer – Think Vegan
Eric Mirbach & Julia Koch – Vegan Good Life
Chris Cooney & Jon Tedd – The Vegan Zombie
Dr Mudar Mannah & Lars Hoffman – Happy Cheeze
Ryan & Angela – Jets Like Taxis & Smash Transit
Vincent Campellone, Dallas Kashuba, Vique Martin
Bram Hubbell, Graham Land, Mark Obstfeld
and all of my Kickstarter backers & recipe testers

The Lotus and the Artichoke

Vegan Recipes from World Adventures

Escape into other culinary worlds with over 100 vegan recipes inspired by my travels & adventures in over 50 countries!

Discover incredible Indo-Chinese delights, Indian feasts, Asian wonders, Italian, French, German and other exciting European classics, amazing African medleys, American family favorites, seductive sweets from around the globe, plus super-charged salads & snacks.

216 pages • €19,90
ISBN 978-3-95575-012-1

Awarded by **Vegetarian Association of Germany (VEBU)**
Top 10 Finalist **Cookbook of the Year 2013**

The Lotus and the Artichoke

MEXICO! A culinary adventure with over 60 vegan recipes

Explore an exciting new world of flavor with my new collection of recipes inspired by 3 months of life & travels in Mexico!

Cross the border with mind-blowing salads & snacks, mouth-watering tacos, incredible enchiladas, tasty tamales & delicious sweets for cooks & food lovers of all kinds.

128 pages • €14
ISBN 978-3-95575-027-5

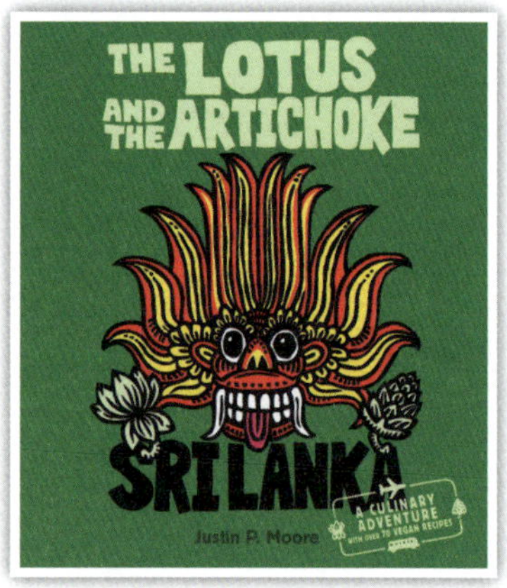

The Lotus and the Artichoke

SRI LANKA – A culinary adventure with over 70 vegan recipes

Taste paradise with this collection of awesome, original recipes inspired by 10 weeks of travels in the land of spice & demons!

Enjoy tropical salads & snacks, legendary short eats, classic curries & exotic desserts you can easily make in your own kitchen.

160 pages • €14
ISBN 978-3-95575-047-3

edition KOCHEN OHNE KNOCHEN
ventil